T0257312

Early praise for *Data Science Essentials in Python*

This book does a fantastic job at summarizing the various activities when wrangling data with Python. Each exercise serves an interesting challenge that is fun to pursue. This book should no doubt be on the reading list of every aspiring data scientist.

➤ **Peter Hampton**
Ulster University

Data Science Essentials in Python gets you up to speed with the most common tasks and tools in the data science field. It's a quick introduction to many different techniques for fetching, cleaning, analyzing, and storing your data. This book helps you stay productive so you can spend less time on technology research and more on your intended research.

➤ **Jason Montojo**
Coauthor of *Practical Programming: An Introduction to Computer Science Using Python 3*

For those who are highly curious and passionate about problem solving and making data discoveries, *Data Science Essentials in Python* provides deep insights and the right set of tools and techniques to start with. Well-drafted examples and exercises make it practical and highly readable.

➤ **Lokesh Kumar Makani**
CASB expert, Skyhigh Networks

Python Companion to Data Science

Collect → Organize → Explore → Predict → Value

Dmitry Zinoviev

The Pragmatic Bookshelf

Raleigh, North Carolina

Many of the designations used by manufacturers and sellers to distinguish their products are claimed as trademarks. Where those designations appear in this book, and The Pragmatic Programmers, LLC was aware of a trademark claim, the designations have been printed in initial capital letters or in all capitals. The Pragmatic Starter Kit, The Pragmatic Programmer, Pragmatic Programming, Pragmatic Bookshelf, PragProg and the linking *g* device are trademarks of The Pragmatic Programmers, LLC.

Every precaution was taken in the preparation of this book. However, the publisher assumes no responsibility for errors or omissions, or for damages that may result from the use of information (including program listings) contained herein.

Our Pragmatic books, screencasts, and audio books can help you and your team create better software and have more fun. Visit us at *https://pragprog.com*.

The team that produced this book includes:

Katharine Dvorak (editor)
Potomac Indexing, LLC (index)
Nicole Abramowitz (copyedit)
Gilson Graphics (layout)
Janet Furlow (producer)

For sales, volume licensing, and support, please contact *support@pragprog.com*.

For international rights, please contact *rights@pragprog.com*.

Copyright © 2016 The Pragmatic Programmers, LLC.
All rights reserved.

No part of this publication may be reproduced, stored in a retrieval system, or transmitted, in any form, or by any means, electronic, mechanical, photocopying, recording, or otherwise, without the prior consent of the publisher.

Printed in the United States of America.
ISBN-13: 978-1-68050-184-1
Printed on acid-free paper.
Book version: P1.0—August 2016

*To my beautiful and most intelligent wife
Anna; to our children: graceful ballerina
Eugenia and romantic gamer Roman; and to
my first data science class of summer 2015.*

Contents

Acknowledgments xi

Preface xiii

1. **What Is Data Science?** **1**
   Unit 1. Data Analysis Sequence 3
   Unit 2. Data Acquisition Pipeline 5
   Unit 3. Report Structure 7
   Your Turn 8

2. **Core Python for Data Science** **9**
   Unit 4. Understanding Basic String Functions 10
   Unit 5. Choosing the Right Data Structure 13
   Unit 6. Comprehending Lists Through List
           Comprehension 15
   Unit 7. Counting with Counters 17
   Unit 8. Working with Files 18
   Unit 9. Reaching the Web 19
   Unit 10. Pattern Matching with Regular Expressions 21
   Unit 11. Globbing File Names and Other Strings 26
   Unit 12. Pickling and Unpickling Data 27
   Your Turn 28

3. **Working with Text Data** **29**
   Unit 13. Processing HTML Files 30
   Unit 14. Handling CSV Files 34
   Unit 15. Reading JSON Files 36
   Unit 16. Processing Texts in Natural Languages 38
   Your Turn 44

4. **Working with Databases** **47**
   Unit 17. Setting Up a MySQL Database 48

Unit 18.   Using a MySQL Database: Command Line   51
Unit 19.   Using a MySQL Database: pymysql   55
Unit 20.   Taming Document Stores: MongoDB   57
Your Turn   61

5.   **Working with Tabular Numeric Data**   63
Unit 21.   Creating Arrays   64
Unit 22.   Transposing and Reshaping   67
Unit 23.   Indexing and Slicing   69
Unit 24.   Broadcasting   71
Unit 25.   Demystifying Universal Functions   73
Unit 26.   Understanding Conditional Functions   75
Unit 27.   Aggregating and Ordering Arrays   76
Unit 28.   Treating Arrays as Sets   78
Unit 29.   Saving and Reading Arrays   79
Unit 30.   Generating a Synthetic Sine Wave   80
Your Turn   82

6.   **Working with Data Series and Frames**   83
Unit 31.   Getting Used to Pandas Data Structures   85
Unit 32.   Reshaping Data   92
Unit 33.   Handling Missing Data   98
Unit 34.   Combining Data   101
Unit 35.   Ordering and Describing Data   105
Unit 36.   Transforming Data   109
Unit 37.   Taming Pandas File I/O   116
Your Turn   119

7.   **Working with Network Data**   121
Unit 38.   Dissecting Graphs   122
Unit 39.   Network Analysis Sequence   126
Unit 40.   Harnessing Networkx   127
Your Turn   134

8.   **Plotting**   135
Unit 41.   Basic Plotting with PyPlot   136
Unit 42.   Getting to Know Other Plot Types   139
Unit 43.   Mastering Embellishments   140
Unit 44.   Plotting with Pandas   143
Your Turn   146

9. **Probability and Statistics** **147**
    Unit 45.   Reviewing Probability Distributions   148
    Unit 46.   Recollecting Statistical Measures   150
    Unit 47.   Doing Stats the Python Way   152
    Your Turn   156

10. **Machine Learning** **157**
    Unit 48.   Designing a Predictive Experiment   158
    Unit 49.   Fitting a Linear Regression   160
    Unit 50.   Grouping Data with K-Means Clustering   166
    Unit 51.   Surviving in Random Decision Forests   169
    Your Turn   171

A1. **Further Reading** **173**
A2. **Solutions to Single-Star Projects** **175**

    Bibliography **185**
    Index **187**

Acknowledgments

I am grateful to Professor Xinxin Jiang (Suffolk University) for his valuable comments on the statistics section of the book, and to Jason Montojo (one of the authors of *Practical Programming: An Introduction to Computer Science Using Python 3*), Amirali Sanatinia (Northeastern University), Peter Hampton (Ulster University), Anuja Kelkar (Carnegie Mellon University), and Lokesh Kumar Makani (Skyhigh Networks) for their indispensable reviews.

I must instruct you in a little science by-and-by, to distract your thoughts.

> *Marie Corelli, British novelist*

Preface

This book was inspired by an introductory data science course in Python that I taught in summer 2015 to a small group of select undergraduate students of Suffolk University in Boston. The course was expected to be the first in a two-course sequence, with an emphasis on obtaining, cleaning, organizing, and visualizing data, sprinkled with some elements of statistics, machine learning, and network analysis.

I quickly came to realize that the abundance of systems and Python modules involved in these operations (databases, natural language processing frameworks, JSON and HTML parsers, and high-performance numerical data structures, to name a few) could easily overwhelm not only an undergraduate student, but also a seasoned professional. In fact, I have to confess that while working on my own research projects in the fields of data science and network analysis, I had to spend more time calling the help() function and browsing scores of online Python discussion boards than I was comfortable with. In addition, I must admit to some embarrassing moments in the classroom when I seemed to have hopelessly forgotten the name of some function or some optional parameter.

As a part of teaching the course, I compiled a set of cheat sheets on various topics that turned out to be a useful reference. The cheat sheets eventually evolved into this book. Hopefully, having it on your desk will make you think more about data science and data analysis than about function names and optional parameters.

About This Book

This book covers data acquisition, cleaning, storing, retrieval, transformation, visualization, elements of advanced data analysis (network analysis), statistics, and machine learning. It is not an introduction to data science or a general data science reference, although you'll find a quick overview of how to do data science in Chapter 1, *What Is Data Science?*, on page 1. I assume that you have learned the methods of data science, including statistics, elsewhere. The subject index at the end of the book refers to the Python implementations of the key concepts, but in most cases you will already be familiar with the concepts.

You'll find a summary of Python data structures; string, file, and web functions; regular expressions; and even list comprehension in Chapter 2, *Core Python for Data Science*, on page 9. This summary is provided to refresh your knowledge of these topics, not to teach them. There are a lot of excellent Python texts, and having a mastery of the language is absolutely important for a successful data scientist.

The first part of the book looks at working with different types of text data, including processing structured and unstructured text, processing numeric data with the NumPy and Pandas modules, and network analysis. Three more chapters address different analysis aspects: working with relational and non-relational databases, data visualization, and simple predictive analysis.

This book is partly a story and partly a reference. Depending on how you see it, you can either read it sequentially or jump right to the index, find the function or concept of concern, and look up relevant explanations and examples. In the former case, if you are an experienced Python programmer, you can safely skip Chapter 2, *Core Python for Data Science*, on page 9. If you do not plan to work with external databases (such as MySQL), you can ignore Chapter 4, *Working with Databases*, on page 47, as well. Lastly, Chapter 9, *Probability and Statistics*, on page 147, assumes that you have no idea about statistics. If you do, you have an excuse to bypass the first two units and find yourself at Unit 47, *Doing Stats the Python Way*, on page 152.

About the Audience

At this point, you may be asking yourself if you want to have this book on your bookshelf.

The book is intended for graduate and undergraduate students, data science instructors, entry-level data science professionals—especially those converting from R to Python—and developers who want a reference to help them remember all of the Python functions and options.

Is that you? If so, *abandon all hesitation and enter.*

About the Software

Despite some controversy surrounding the transition from Python 2.7 to Python 3.3 and above, I firmly stand behind the newer Python dialect. Most new Python software is developed for 3.3, and most of the legacy software has been successfully ported to 3.3, too. Considering the trend, it would be unwise to choose an outdated dialect, no matter how popular it may seem at the time.

All Python examples in this book are known to work for the modules mentioned in the following table. All of these modules, with the exception of the community module that must be installed separately[1] and the Python interpreter itself, are included in the Anaconda distribution, which is provided by Continuum Analytics and is available for free.[2]

Package	Used version	Package	Used version
BeautifulSoup	4.3.2	community	0.3
json	2.0.9	html5lib	0.999
matplotlib	1.4.3	networkx	1.10.0
nltk	3.1.0	numpy	1.10.1
pandas	0.17.0	pymongo	3.0.2
pymysql	0.6.2	python	3.4.3
scikit-learn	0.16.1	scipy	0.16.0

Table 1—Software Components Used in the Book

If you plan to experiment (or actually work) with databases, you will also need to download and install MySQL[3] and MongoDB.[4] Both databases are free and known to work on Linux, Mac OS, and Windows platforms.

Notes on Quotes

Python allows the user to enclose character strings in 'single', "double", "'triple'", and even """triple double""" quotes (the latter two can be used for multiline strings). However, when printing out strings, it always uses single quote notation, regardless of which quotes you used in the program.

Many other languages (C, C++, Java) use single and double quotes differently: single for individual characters, double for character strings. To pay tribute

---

1. pypi.python.org/pypi/python-louvain/0.3
2. www.continuum.io
3. www.mysql.com
4. www.mongodb.com

to this differentiation, in this book I, too, use single quotes for single characters and double quotes for character strings.

The Book Forum

The community forum for this book can be found online at the Pragmatic Programmers web page for this book.[5] There you can ask questions, post comments, and submit errata.

Another great resource for questions and answers (not specific to this book) is the newly created Data Science Stack Exchange forum.[6]

Your Turn

The end of each chapter features a unit called "Your Turn." This unit has descriptions of several projects that you may want to accomplish on your own (or with someone you trust) to strengthen your understanding of the material.

The projects marked with a single star[*] are the simplest. All you need to work on them is solid knowledge of the functions mentioned in the preceding chapters. Expect to complete single-star projects in no more than thirty minutes. You'll find solutions to them in Appendix 2, *Solutions to Single-Star Projects*, on page 175.

The projects marked with two stars[**] are hard(er). They may take you an hour or more, depending on your programming skills and habits. Two-star projects involve the use of intermediate data structures and well thought-out algorithms.

Finally, the three-star[***] projects are the hardest. Some of the three-star projects may not even have a perfect solution, so don't get desperate if you cannot find one! Just by working on these projects, you certainly make yourself a better programmer and a better data scientist. And if you're an educator, think of the three-star projects as potential mid-semester assignments.

Now, let's get started!

Dmitry Zinoviev
dzinoviev@gmail.com
August 2016

---

5. pragprog.com/book/dzpyds
6. datascience.stackexchange.com

CHAPTER 1

What Is Data Science?

I'm sure you already have an idea about what data science is, but it never hurts to remind! Data science is the discipline of the extraction of knowledge from data. It relies on computer science (for data structures, algorithms, visualization, big data support, and general programming), statistics (for regressions and inference), and domain knowledge (for asking questions and interpreting results).

Data science traditionally concerns itself with a number of dissimilar topics, some of which you may be already familiar with and some of which you'll encounter in this book:

- *Databases*, which provide information storage and integration. You'll find information about relational databases and document stores in Chapter 4, *Working with Databases*, on page 47.

- *Text analysis* and *natural language processing*, which let us "compute with words" by translating qualitative text into quantitative variables. Interested in tools for sentiment analysis? Look no further than Unit 16, *Processing Texts in Natural Languages*, on page 38.

- *Numeric data analysis* and *data mining*, which search for consistent patterns and relationships between variables. These are the subjects of Chapter 5, *Working with Tabular Numeric Data*, on page 63 and Chapter 6, *Working with Data Series and Frames*, on page 83.

- *Complex network analysis*, which is not complex at all. It is about complex networks: collections of arbitrary interconnected entities. Chapter 7, *Working with Network Data*, on page 121, makes complex network analysis simpler.

- *Data visualization*, which is not just cute but is extremely useful, especially when it comes to persuading your data sponsor to sponsor you again. If one picture is worth a thousand words, then Chapter 8, *Plotting*, on page 135, is worth the rest of the book.

- *Machine learning* (including clustering, decision trees, classification, and neural networks), which attempts to get computers to "think" and make predictions based on sample data. Chapter 10, *Machine Learning*, on page 157, explains how.

- *Time series processing* and, more generally, *digital signal processing*, which are indispensable tools for stock market analysts, economists, and researchers in audio and video domains.

- *Big data analysis*, which typically refers to the analysis of unstructured data (text, audio, video) in excess of one terabyte, produced and captured at high frequency. Big data is simply too big to fit in this book, too.

Regardless of the analysis type, data science is firstly science and only then sorcery. As such, it is a process that follows a pretty rigorous basic sequence that starts with data acquisition and ends with a report of the results. In this chapter, you'll take a look at the basic processes of data science: the steps of a typical data analysis study, where to acquire data, and the structure of a typical project report.

Data Analysis Sequence

The steps of a typical data analysis study are generally consistent with a general scientific discovery sequence.

Your data science discovery starts with the question to be answered and the type of analysis to be applied. The simplest analysis type is *descriptive*, where the data set is described by reporting its aggregate measures, often in a visual form. No matter what you do next, you have to at least describe the data! During *exploratory* data analysis, you try to find new relationships between existing variables. If you have a small data sample and would like to describe a bigger population, statistics-based *inferential* analysis is right for you. A *predictive* analyst learns from the past to predict the future. *Causal* analysis identifies variables that affect each other. Finally, *mechanistic* data analysis explores exactly how one variable affects another variable.

However, your analysis is only as good as the data you use. What is the ideal data set? What data has the answer to your question in an ideal world? By the way, the ideal data set may not exist at all or be hard or infeasible to obtain. Things happen, but perhaps a smaller or not so feature-rich data set would still work?

Fortunately, getting the raw data from the web or from a database is not that hard, and there are plenty of Python tools that assist with downloading and deciphering it. You'll take a closer look in Unit 2, *Data Acquisition Pipeline*, on page 5.

In this imperfect world, there is no perfect data. "Dirty" data has missing values, outliers, and other "non-standard" items. Some examples of "dirty" data are birth dates in the future, negative ages and weights, and email addresses not intended for use (noreply@). Once you obtain the raw data, the next step is to use data-cleaning tools and your knowledge of statistics to regularize the data set.

With clean data in your files, you then perform descriptive and exploratory analysis. The output of this step often includes scatter plots (mentioned on page 143), histograms, and statistical summaries (explained on page 150). They give you a smell and sense of data—an intuition that is indispensable for further research, especially if the data set has many dimensions.

And now you are just one step away from prognosticating. Your tools of the trade are data models that, if properly trained, can learn from the past and predict the future. Don't forget about assessing the quality of the constructed models and their prediction accuracy!

At this point you take your statistician and programmer hats off and put a domain expert hat on. You've got some results, but are they domain-significant? In other words, does anyone care about them and do they make any difference? Pretend that you're a reviewer hired to evaluate your own work. What did you do right, what did you do wrong, and what would you do better or differently if you had another chance? Would you use different data, run different types of analysis, ask a different question, or build a different model? Someone is going to ask these questions—it's better if you ask them first. Start looking for the answers when you are still deeply immersed in the context.

Last, but not least, you have to produce a report that explains how and why you processed the data, what models were built, and what conclusions and predictions are possible. You'll take a look at the report structure at the end of this chapter in Unit 3, *Report Structure*, on page 7.

As your companion to select areas of data science in the Python language, this book's focus is mainly on the earlier, least formalized, and most creative steps of a typical data analysis sequence: getting, cleaning, organizing, and sizing the data. Data modeling, including predictive data modeling, is barely touched. (It would be unfair to leave data modeling out completely, because that's where the real magic happens!) In general, results interpretation, challenging, and reporting are very domain-specific and belong to specialized texts.

Data Acquisition Pipeline

Data acquisition is all about obtaining the artifacts that contain the input data from a variety of sources, extracting the data from the artifacts, and converting it into representations suitable for further processing, as shown in the following figure.

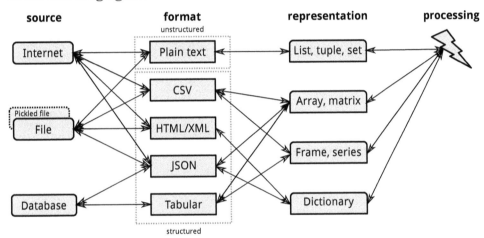

The three main sources of data are the Internet (namely, the World Wide Web), databases, and local files (possibly previously downloaded by hand or using additional software). Some of the local files may have been produced by other Python programs and contain serialized or "pickled" data (see Unit 12, *Pickling and Unpickling Data*, on page 27, for further explanation).

The formats of data in the artifacts may range widely. In the chapters that follow, you'll consider ways and means of working with the most popular formats:

- Unstructured plain text in a natural language (such as English or Chinese)
- Structured data, including:
  - Tabular data in comma separated values (CSV) files
  - Tabular data from databases
  - Tagged data in HyperText Markup Language (HTML) or, in general, in eXtensible Markup Language (XML)
  - Tagged data in JavaScript Object Notation (JSON)

Depending on the original structure of the extracted data and the purpose and nature of further processing, the data used in the examples in this book are represented using native Python data structures (lists and dictionaries) or advanced data structures that support specialized operations (numpy arrays and pandas data frames).

I attempt to keep the data processing pipeline (obtaining, cleaning, and transforming raw data; descriptive and exploratory data analysis; and data modeling and prediction) fully automated. For this reason, I avoid using interactive GUI tools, as they can rarely be scripted to operate in a batch mode, and they rarely record any history of operations. To promote modularity, reusability, and recoverability, I'll break a long pipeline into shorter sub-pipelines, saving intermediate results into Pickle (on page 27) or JSON (on page 36) files, as appropriate.

Pipeline automation naturally leads to reproducible code: a set of Python scripts that anyone can execute to convert the original raw data into the final results as described in the report, ideally without any additional human interaction. Other researchers can use reproducible code to validate your models and results and to apply the process that you developed to their own problems.

Unit 3

Report Structure

The project report is what we (data scientists) submit to the data sponsor (the customer). The report typically includes the following:

- Abstract (a brief and accessible description of the project)

- Introduction

- Methods that were used for data acquisition and processing

- Results that were obtained (do not include intermediate and insignificant results in this section; rather, put them into an appendix)

- Conclusion

- Appendix

In addition to the non-essential results and graphics, the appendix contains all reproducible code used to process the data: well-commented scripts that can be executed without any command-line parameters and user interaction.

The last but not least important part of the submission is the raw data: any data file that is required to execute the code in a reproducible way, unless the file has been provided by the data sponsor and has not been changed. A README file typically explains the provenance of the data and the format of every attached data file.

Take this structure as a recommendation, not something cast in stone. Your data sponsor and common sense may suggest an alternative implementation.

Your Turn

In this introductory chapter, you looked at the basic processes of data science: the steps in a typical data analysis study, where to obtain data and the different formats of data, and the structure of a typical project report. The rest of the book introduces the features of Python that are essential to elementary data science, as well as various Python modules that provide algorithmic and statistical support for a data science project of modest complexity.

Before you continue, let's do a simple project to get our Python feet wet. (Do pythons have feet?) Computer programmers have a good tradition of introducing beginners to a new programming language by writing a program that outputs "Hello, World!" There is no reason for us not to follow the rule.

Hello, World![*]

Write a program that outputs "Hello, World!" (less the quotes) on the Python command line.

And I spoke to them in as many languages as I had the least smattering of, which were High and Low Dutch, Latin, French, Spanish, Italian, and Lingua Franca, but all to no purpose.

— *Jonathan Swift, Anglo-Irish satirist*

CHAPTER 2

Core Python for Data Science

Some features of the core Python language are more important for data analysis than others. In this chapter, you'll look at the most essential of them: string functions, data structures, list comprehension, counters, file and web functions, regular expressions, globbing, and data pickling. You'll learn how to use Python to extract data from local disk files and the Internet, store them into appropriate data structures, locate bits and pieces matching certain patterns, and serialize and de-serialize Python objects for future processing. However, these functions are by no means specific to data science or data analysis tasks and are found in many other applications.

It's a common misunderstanding that the presence of high-level programming tools makes low-level programming obsolete. With the Anaconda distribution of Python alone providing more than 350 Python packages, who needs to split strings and open files? The truth is, there are at least as many non-standard data sources in the world as those that follow the rules.

All standard data frames, series, CSV readers, and word tokenizers follow the rules set up by their creators. They fail miserably when they come across anything out of compliance with the rules. That's when you blow the dust off this book and demote yourself from glorified data scientist to humble but very useful computer programmer.

You may need to go as far "down" as to the string functions—in fact, they are just around the corner on page 10.

Unit 4

Understanding Basic String Functions

A string is a basic unit of interaction between the world of computers and the world of humans. Initially, almost all raw data is stored as strings. In this unit, you'll learn how to assess and manipulate text strings.

All functions described in this unit are members of the str built-in class.

The *case conversion* functions return a copy of the original string s: lower() converts all characters to lowercase; upper() converts all characters to uppercase; and capitalize() converts the first character to uppercase and all other characters to lowercase. These functions don't affect non-alphabetic characters. Case conversion functions are an important element of normalization, which you'll look at on page 41.

The *predicate* functions return True or False, depending on whether the string s belongs to the appropriate class: islower() checks if all alphabetic characters are in lowercase; isupper() checks if all alphabetic characters are in uppercase; isspace() checks if all characters are spaces; isdigit() checks if all characters are decimal digits in the range 0–9; and isalpha() checks if all characters are alphabetic characters in the ranges a–z or A–Z. You will use these functions to recognize valid words, nonnegative integer numbers, punctuation, and the like.

Sometimes Python represents string data as raw binary arrays, not as character strings, especially when the data came from an external source: an external file, a database, or the web. Python uses the b notation for binary arrays. For example, bin = b"Hello" is a binary array; s = "Hello" is a string. Respectively, s[0] is 'H' and bin[0] is 72, where 72 is the ASCII charcode for the character 'H'. The *decoding* functions convert a binary array to a character string and back: bin.decode() converts a binary array to a string, and s.encode() converts a string to a binary array. Many Python functions expect that binary data is converted to strings until it is further processed.

The first step toward string processing is getting rid of unwanted whitespaces (including new lines and tabs). The functions lstrip() (left strip), rstrip() (right strip), and strip() remove all whitespaces at the beginning, at the end, or all around the string. (They don't remove the inner spaces.) With all these removals, you should be prepared to end up with an empty string!

```
"   Hello,   world!   \t\t\n".strip()
```

⇒ `'Hello,   world!'`

Often a string consists of several tokens, separated by delimiters such as spaces, colons, and commas. The function split(delim='') splits the string s into a list of substrings, using delim as the delimiter. If the delimiter isn't specified, Python splits the string by all whitespaces and lumps all contiguous whitespaces together:

```
"Hello,   world!".split() # Two spaces!
```

⇒ `['Hello,', 'world!']`

```
"Hello,   world!".split(" ") # Two spaces!
```

⇒ `['Hello,', '', 'world!']`

```
"www.networksciencelab.com".split(".")
```

⇒ `['www', 'networksciencelab', 'com']`

The sister function join(ls) joins a list of strings ls into one string, using the object string as the glue. You can recombine fragments with join():

```
", ".join(["alpha", "bravo", "charlie", "delta"])
```

⇒ `'alpha, bravo, charlie, delta'`

In the previous example, join() inserts the glue only between the strings and not in front of the first string or after the last string. The result of splitting a string and joining the fragments again is often indistinguishable from replacing the split delimiter with the glue:

```
"-".join("1.617.305.1985".split("."))
```

⇒ `'1-617-305-1985'`

Sometimes you may want to use the two functions together to remove unwanted whitespaces from a string. You can accomplish the same effect by regular expression-based substitution (which you'll look at later on page 25).

```
" ".join("This string\n\r  has    many\t\tspaces".split())
```

⇒ `'This string has many spaces'`

The function find(needle) returns the index of the first occurrence of the substring needle in the object string or -1 if the substring is not present. This function is case-sensitive. It is used to find a fragment of interest in a string —if it exists.

```
"www.networksciencelab.com".find(".com")
```

⇒ **21**

The function count(needle) returns the number of non-overlapping occurrences of the substring needle in the object string. This function is also case-sensitive.

```
"www.networksciencelab.com".count(".")
```

⇒ **2**

Strings are an important building block of any data-processing program, but not the only building block—and not the most efficient building block, either. You will also use lists, tuples, sets, and dictionaries to bundle string and numeric data and enable efficient searching and sorting.

Unit 5

Choosing the Right Data Structure

The most commonly used compound data structures in Python are lists, tuples, sets, and dictionaries. All four of them are collections.

Python implements *lists* as arrays. They have linear search time, which makes them impractical for storing large amounts of searchable data.

Tuples are immutable lists. Once created, they cannot be changed. They still have linear search time.

Unlike lists and tuples, *sets* are not sequences: set items don't have indexes. Sets can store at most one copy of an item and have sublinear O(log(N)) search time. They are excellent for membership look-ups and eliminating duplicates (if you convert a list with duplicates to a set, the duplicates are gone):

```
myList = list(set(myList)) # Remove duplicates from myList
```

You can transform list data to a set for faster membership look-ups. For example, let's say bigList is a list of the first 10 million integer numbers represented as decimal strings:

```
bigList = [str(i) for i in range(10000000)]
"abc" in bigList # Takes 0.2 sec
bigSet = set(bigList)
"abc" in bigSet # Takes 15–30 μsec–10000 times faster!
```

Dictionaries map keys to values. An object of any hashable data type (number, Boolean, string, tuple) can be a key, and different keys in the same dictionary can belong to different data types. There is no restriction on the data types of dictionary values. Dictionaries have sublinear O(log(N)) search time. They are excellent for key-value look-ups.

You can create a dictionary from a list of (key, value) tuples, and you can use a built-in class constructor enumerate(seq) to create a dictionary where the key is the sequence number of an item in seq:

```
seq = ["alpha", "bravo", "charlie", "delta"]
dict(enumerate(seq))
```

⇒ **{0: 'alpha', 1: 'bravo', 2: 'charlie', 3: 'delta'}**

Another smart way to create a dictionary from a sequence of keys (kseq) and a sequence of values (vsec) is through a built-in class constructor, zip(kseq, vseq) (the sequences must be of the same length):

```
kseq = "abcd" # A string is a sequence, too
vseq = ["alpha", "bravo", "charlie", "delta"]
dict(zip(kseq, vseq))
```

⇒ **{'a': 'alpha', 'c': 'charlie', 'b': 'bravo', 'd': 'delta'}**

Python implements enumerate(seq) and zip(kseq, vseq) (and the good old range(), too) as list generators. List generators provide an iterator interface, which makes it possible to use them in for loops. Unlike a real list, a list generator produces the next element in a lazy way, only as needed. Generators facilitate working with large lists and even permit "infinite" lists. You can explicitly coerce a generator to a list by calling the list() function.

Unit 6

Comprehending Lists Through List Comprehension

List comprehension is an expression that transforms a collection (not necessarily a list) into a list. It is used to apply the same operation to all or some list elements, such as converting all elements to uppercase or raising them all to a power.

The transformation process looks like this:

1. The expression iterates over the collection and visits the items from the collection.

2. An optional Boolean expression (default True) is evaluated for each item.

3. If the Boolean expression is True, the loop expression is evaluated for the current item, and its value is appended to the result list.

4. If the Boolean expression is False, the item is ignored.

Here are some trivial list comprehensions:

```
# Copy myList; same as myList.copy() or myList[:], but less efficient
[x for x in myList]
# Extract non-negative items
[x for x in myList if x >= 0]
# Build a list of squares
[x**2 for x in myList]
# Build a list of valid reciprocals
[1/x for x in myList if x != 0]
# Collect all non-empty lines from the open file infile,
# with trailing and leading whitespaces removed
[l.strip() for l in infile if l.strip()]
```

In the latter example, the function strip() is evaluated twice for each list item. If you don't want the duplication, you can use nested list comprehensions. The inner one strips off the whitespaces, and the outer one eliminates empty strings:

```
[line for line in [l.strip() for l in infile] if line]
```

If you enclose a list comprehension in parentheses rather than in square brackets, it evaluates to a list generator object:

```
(x**2 for x in myList) # Evaluates to <generator object <genexpr> at 0x...>
```

Often the result of list comprehension is a list of repeating items: numbers, words, word stems, and lemmas. You want to know which item is the most or least common. Counter class, coming up next in Unit 7, *Counting with Counters*, on page 17, is a poor man's tool for collecting these sorts of statistics.

Unit 7

Counting with Counters

A counter is a dictionary-style collection for tallying items in another collection. It is defined in the module collections. You can pass the collection to be tallied to the constructor Counter and then use the function most_common(n) to get a list of n most frequent items and their frequencies (if you don't provide n, the function will return a list of all items).

```
from collections import Counter
phrase = "a man a plan a canal panama"
cntr = Counter(phrase.split())
cntr.most_common()
```

⇒ `[('a', 3), ('canal', 1), ('panama', 1), ('plan', 1), ('man', 1)]`

The latter list can be converted to a dictionary for easy look-ups:

```
cntrDict = dict(cntr.most_common())
```

⇒ `{'a': 3, 'canal': 1, 'panama': 1, 'plan': 1, 'man': 1}`

```
cntrDict['a']
```

⇒ **3**

You'll look at more versatile, pandas-base counting tools in the unit *Uniqueness, Counting, Membership*, on page 108.

Working with Files

A file is a non-volatile container for long-term data storage. A typical file operation involves opening a file, reading data from the file or writing data into the file, and closing the file. You can open a file for reading (default mode, denoted as "r"), [over]writing ("w"), or appending ("a"). Opening a file for writing destroys the original content of the file without notice, and opening a non-existing file for reading causes an exception:

```
f = open(name, mode="r")
«read the file»
f.close()
```

Python provides an efficient replacement to this paradigm: the with statement allows us to open a file explicitly, but it lets Python close the file automatically after exiting, thus saving us from tracking the unwanted open files.

```
with open(name, mode="r") as f:
  «read the file»
```

Some modules, such as pickle (discussed in Unit 12, *Pickling and Unpickling Data*, on page 27), require that a file be opened in binary mode ("rb", "wb", or "ab"). You should also use binary mode for reading/writing raw binary arrays. The following functions read text data from a previously opened file f:

```
f.read() # Read all data as a string or a binary
f.read(n) # Read the first n bytes as a string or a binary
f.readline() # Read the next line as a string
f.readlines() # Read all lines as a list of strings
```

You can mix and match these functions, as needed. For example, you can read the first string, then the next five bytes, then the next line, and finally the rest of the file. The newline character is not removed from the results returned by any of these functions. Generally, it is unsafe to use the functions read() and readlines() if you cannot assume that the file size is reasonably small.

The following functions write text data to a previously opened file f:

```
f.write(line) # Write a string or a binary
f.writelines(ines) # Write a list of strings
```

These functions don't add a newline character at the end of the written strings —that's your responsibility.

Reaching the Web

According to WorldWideWebSize,[1] the indexed web contains at least 4.85 billion pages. Some of them may be of interest to us. The module urllib.request contains functions for downloading data from the web. While it may be feasible (though not advisable) to download a single data set by hand, save it into the cache directory, and then analyze it using Python scripts, some data analysis projects call for automated iterative or recursive downloads.

The first step toward getting anything off the web is to open the URL with the function urlopen(url) and obtain the open URL handle. Once opened, the URL handle is similar to a read-only open file handle: you can use the functions read(), readline(), and readlines() to access the data.

Due to the dynamic nature of the web and the Internet, the likelihood of failing to open a URL is higher than that of opening a local disk file. Remember to enclose any call to a web-related function in an exception handling statement:

```
import urllib.request
try:
  with urllib.request.urlopen("http://www.networksciencelab.com") as doc:
    html = doc.read()
    # If reading was successful, the connection is closed automatically
except:
  print("Could not open %s" % doc, file=sys.err)
  # Do not pretend that the document has been read!
  # Execute an error handler here
```

If the data set of interest is deployed at a website that requires authentication, urlopen() will not work. Instead, use a module that provides Secure Sockets Layer (SSL; for example, OpenSSL).

The module urllib.parse supplies friendly tools for parsing and unparsing (building) URLs. The function urlparse() splits a URL into a tuple of six elements: scheme (such as http), network address, file system path, parameters, query, and fragment:

---

1. www.worldwidewebsize.com

```
import urllib.parse
URL = "http://networksciencelab.com/index.html;param?foo=bar#content"
urllib.parse.urlparse(URL)
```

⇒ **ParseResult(scheme='http', netloc='networksciencelab.com',**
⇒   **path='/index.html', params='param', query='foo=bar',**
⇒   **fragment='content')**

The function urlunparse(parts) constructs a valid URL from the parts returned by urlparse(). If you parse a URL and then unparse it again, the result may be slightly different from the original URL—but functionally fully equivalent.

Unit 10

Pattern Matching with Regular Expressions

Regular expressions are a powerful mechanism for searching, splitting, and replacing strings based on pattern matching. The module re provides a pattern description language and a collection of functions for matching, searching, splitting, and replacing strings.

From the Python point of view, a regular expression is simply a string containing the description of a pattern. You can make pattern matching much more efficient if you compile a regular expression that you plan to use more than once:

```
compiledPattern = re.compile(pattern, flags=0)
```

Compilation substantially improves pattern matching time but doesn't affect correctness. If you want, you can specify pattern matching flags, either at the time of compilation or later at the time of execution. The most common flags are re.I (ignores character case) and re.M (tells re to work in a multiline mode, and lets the operators ^ and $ also match the start or end of line). If you want to combine several flags, simply add them.

Understanding Regular Expression Language

The regular expression language is partially summarized in the following table.

Basic operators	
.	Any character except newline
a	The character a itself
ab	The string ab itself
x|y	x or y
\y	Escapes a special character y, such as ^+{}$()[]|\-?.*
Character classes	
[a-d]	One character of: a,b,c,d
[^a-d]	One character except: a,b,c,d
\d	One digit
\D	One non-digit
\s	One whitespace
\S	One non-whitespace

\w	One alphanumeric character
\W	One non-alphanumeric character
Quantifiers	
x*	Zero or more xs
x+	One or more xs
x?	Zero or one x
x{2}	Exactly two xs
x{2,5}	Between two and five xs
Escaped characters	
\n	Newline
\r	Carriage return
\t	Tab
Assertions	
^	Start of string
\b	Word boundary
\B	Non-word boundary
$	End of string
Groups	
(x)	Capturing group
(?:x)	Non-capturing group

Table 2—Regular Expression Language

The caret (^) and dash (-) operators in the middle or at the end of a character class expression don't have a special meaning and represent characters '^' and '-'. Groups change the order of operations. Substrings that match capturing groups are also included in the list of results, when appropriate.

Note that regular expressions make extensive use of backslashes ('\'). A backslash is an escape character in Python. To be treated as a regular character, it must be preceded by another backslash ('\\'), which results in clumsy regular expressions with endless pairs of backslashes. Python supports raw strings where backslashes are not interpreted as escape characters.

To define a raw string, put the character r immediately in front of the opening quotation mark. The following two strings are equal, and neither of them contains a newline character:

```
"\\n"
r"\n"
```

You will always write regular expressions as raw strings.

Now it's time to have a look at some useful regular expressions. The purpose of these examples is not to scare you off, but to remind you that life is hard, computer science is harder, and pattern matching is the hardest.

r"\w[-\w\.]*@\w[-\w]*(\.\w[-\w]*)+"
> An email address.

r"<TAG\b[^>]*<(.*?)</TAG>"
> Specific HTML tag with a matching closing tag.

r"[-+]?((\d*\.?\d+)|(\d\.))([eE][-+]?\d+)?"
> A floating point number.

It's tempting to write a regular expression that matches a valid URL, but this is notoriously hard. Bravely resist the temptation and use the module urllib.parse, which was explained earlier on page 19, to parse URLs.

Irregular Regular Expressions

 Python regular expressions are not the only kind of regular expressions on the block. The Perl language uses regular expressions with different syntax and somewhat different semantics (but the same expressive power). In some simple cases (like file name matching), you can use the glob module, discussed in Unit 11, *Globbing File Names and Other Strings*, on page 26, which is yet another type of regular expression.

Searching, Splitting, and Replacing with Module re

Once you write and compile a regular expression, you can use it for splitting, matching, searching, and replacing substrings. The module re provides all necessary functions, and most functions accept patterns in two forms: raw and compiled.

```
re.function(rawPattern, ...)
compiledPattern.function(...)
```

The function split(pattern, string, maxsplit=0, flags=0) splits a string into at most maxsplit substrings by the pattern and returns the list of substrings (if maxsplit==0, all substrings are returned). You can use it, among other things, as a poor man's word tokenizer for word analysis:

```
re.split(r"\W", "Hello, world!")
```

⇒ `['Hello', '', 'world', '']`

```
# Combine all adjacent non-letters
re.split(r"\W+", "Hello, world!")
```

⇒ `['Hello', 'world', '']`

The function match(pattern, string, flags=0) checks if the beginning of a string matches the regular expression. The function returns a match object or None if the match was not found. The matching object, if any, has the functions start(), end(), and group() that return the start and end indexes of the matching fragment, and the fragment itself.

```
mo = re.match(r"\d+", "067 Starts with a number")
```

⇒ `<_sre.SRE_Match object; span=(0, 3), match='067'>`

```
mo.group()
```

⇒ `'067'`

```
re.match(r"\d+", "Does not start with a number")
```

⇒ **None**

The function search(pattern, string, flags=0) checks if any part of a string matches the regular expression. The function returns a match object or None if the match was not found. Use this function instead of match() if the matching fragment is not expected to be at the beginning of a string.

```
re.search(r"[a-z]+", "0010010 Has at least one 010 letter 0010010", re.I)
```

⇒ `<_sre.SRE_Match object; span=(8, 11), match='Has'>`

```
# Case-sensitive version
re.search(r"[a-z]+", "0010010 Has at least one 010 letter 0010010")
```

⇒ `<_sre.SRE_Match object; span=(9, 11), match='as'>`

The function findall(pattern, string, flags=0) finds all substrings that match the regular expression. The function returns a list of substrings. (The list, of course, can be empty.)

```
re.findall(r"[a-z]+", "0010010 Has at least one 010 letter 0010010", re.I)
```

⇒ `['Has', 'at', 'least', 'one', 'letter']`

Capturing vs. Non-Capturing Groups

A non-capturing group is simply a part of a regular expression that re treats as a single token. The parentheses enclosing a non-capturing group serve the same purpose as the parentheses in arithmetic expressions. For example, r"cab+" matches a substring that starts with a "ca", followed by at least one "b", but r"c(?:ab)+" matches a substring that starts with a "c", followed by one or more "ab"s. Note that there are no spaces between "(?:" and the rest of the regular expression.

A capturing group, in addition to grouping, also delineates the substring returned by search() or findall(): r"c(ab)+" describes at least one "ab" after a "c", but only the "ab"s are returned.

The function sub(pattern, repl, string, flags=0) replaces all non-overlapping matching parts of a string with repl. You can restrict the number of replacements with the optional parameter count.

```
re.sub(r"[a-z ]+", "[...]", "0010010 has at least one 010 letter 0010010")
```

⇒ `'0010010[...]010[...]0010010'`

Regular expressions are great, but in many cases (for example, when it comes to matching file names by extension) they are simply too powerful, and you can accomplish comparable results by globbing, which you'll look at how to do in the next unit.

Globbing File Names and Other Strings

Globbing is the process of matching specific file names and wildcards, which are simplified regular expressions. A wildcard may contain the special symbols '*' (represents zero or more characters) and '?' (represents exactly one character). Note that '\', '+', and '.' are not special symbols!

The module glob provides a namesake function for matching wildcards. The function returns a list of all file names that match the wildcard passed as the parameter:

```
glob.glob("*.txt")
```

⇒ `['public.policy.txt', 'big.data.txt']`

The wildcard '*' matches all file names in the current directory (folder), except for those that start with a period ('.'). To match the special file names, use the wildcard ".*".

Unit 12

Pickling and Unpickling Data

The module pickle implements *serialization*—saving arbitrary Python data structures into a file and reading them back as a Python expression. You can read a pickled expression from the file with any Python program, but not with a program written in another language (unless an implementation of the pickle protocol exists in that language).

You must open a pickle file for reading or writing in binary mode:

```
# Dump an object into a file
with open("myData.pickle", "wb") as oFile:
  pickle.dump(object, oFile)

# Load the same object back
with open("myData.pickle", "rb") as iFile:
  object = pickle.load(iFile)
```

You can store more than one object in a pickle file. The function load() either returns the next object from a pickle file or raises an exception if the end of the file is detected. You can also use pickle to store intermediate data processing results that are unlikely to be processed by software with no access to pickle.

Your Turn

In this chapter, you looked at how to extract data from local disk files and the Internet, store them into appropriate data structures, extract bits and pieces matching certain patterns, and pickle for future processing. There is nothing infinite in computer science, but there is an infinite number of scenarios requiring data extraction, broadly ranging in type, purpose, and complexity. Here are just some of them.

*Word Frequency Counter**

Write a program that downloads a web page requested by the user and reports up to ten most frequently used words. The program should treat all words as case-insensitive. For the purpose of this exercise, assume that a word is described by the regular expression r"\w+".

*File Indexer***

Write a program that indexes all files in a certain user-designated directory (folder). The program should construct a dictionary where the keys are all unique words in all the files (as described by the regular expression r"\w+"; treat the words as case-insensitive), and the value of each entry is a list of file names that contain the word. For instance, if the word "aloha" is mentioned in the files "early-internet.dat" and "hawaiian-travel.txt," the dictionary will have an entry {…, 'aloha': ['early-internet.dat', 'hawaiian-travel.txt'], …}.

The program will pickle the dictionary for future use.

*Phone Number Extractor****

Write a program that extracts all phone numbers from a given text file. This is not an easy task, as there are several dozens of national conventions for writing phone numbers (see en.wikipedia.org/wiki/National_conventions_for_writing_telephone_numbers). Can you design one regular expression that catches them all?

And if you thought that this wasn't that hard, try extracting postal addresses!

Who was this Jason, and why did the gods favor him so?
Where did he come from, and what was his story?

> Homer, Greek poet

## CHAPTER 3

Working with Text Data

Often raw data comes from all kinds of text documents: structured documents (HTML, XML, CSV, and JSON files) or unstructured documents (plain, human-readable text). As a matter of fact, unstructured text is perhaps the hardest data source to work with because the processing software has to infer the meaning of the data items.

All data representations mentioned in the previous paragraph are human-readable. (That's what makes them text documents.) If necessary, we can open any text file in a simple text editor (Notepad on Windows, gedit on Linux, TextEdit on Mac OS X) and read it with our bare eyes or edit it by hand. If no other tools are available, we could treat text documents as texts, regardless of the representation scheme, and explore them using core Python string functions (as discussed in Unit 4, *Understanding Basic String Functions*, on page 10).

Fortunately, Anaconda supplies several excellent modules—BeautifulSoup, csv, json, and nltk—that make the daunting work of text analysis almost exciting. Following the *Occam's razor* principle—*Entities must not be multiplied beyond necessity* (which was actually formulated by John Punch, not by Occam)—we should avoid reinventing existing tools. This is true not just for text-processing tools, but for any Anaconda package.

Let's start working with text data by looking at the simple case of structured data. You'll then figure out how to add some structure to the unstructured text via natural language processing techniques.

Unit 13

Processing HTML Files

The first type of structured text document you'll look at is HTML—a markup language commonly used on the web for human-readable representation of information. An HTML document consists of text and predefined tags (enclosed in angle brackets <>) that control the presentation and interpretation of the text. The tags may have attributes. The following table shows some HTML tags and their attributes.

Tag	Attributes	Purpose
HTML		Whole HTML document
HEAD		Document header
TITLE		Document title
BODY	background, bgcolor	Document body
H1, H2, H3, etc.		Section headers
I, EM		Emphasis
B, STRONG		Strong emphasis
PRE		Preformatted text
P, SPAN, DIV		Paragraph, span, division
BR		Line break
A	href	Hyperlink
IMG	src, width, height	Image
TABLE	width, border	Table
TR		Table row
TH, TD		Table header/data cell
OL, UL		Numbered/itemized list
LI		List item
DL		Description list
DT, DD		Description topic, definition
INPUT	name	User input field
SELECT	name	Pull-down menu

Table 3—Some Frequently Used HTML Tags and Attributes

HTML is a precursor to XML, which is not a language but rather a family of markup languages having similar structure and intended in the first place for machine-readable documents. Users like us define XML tags and their attributes as needed.

XML ≠ HTML

Though XML and HTML look similar, a typical HTML document is in general not a valid XML document, and an XML document is not an HTML document.

XML tags are application-specific. Any alphanumeric string can be a tag, as long as it follows some simple rules (enclosed in angle brackets and so on). XML tags don't control the presentation of the text—only its interpretation. XML is frequently used in documents not intended directly for human eyes. Another language, eXtensible Stylesheet Language Transformation (XSLT), transforms XML to HTML, and yet another language, Cascading Style Sheets (CSS), adds style to resulting HTML documents.

The module BeautifulSoup is used for parsing, accessing, and modifying HTML and XML documents. You can construct a BeautifulSoup object from a markup string, a markup file, or a URL of a markup document on the web:

```
from bs4 import BeautifulSoup
from urllib.request import urlopen

# Construct soup from a string
soup1 = BeautifulSoup("<HTML><HEAD>«headers»</HEAD>«body»</HTML>")

# Construct soup from a local file
soup2 = BeautifulSoup(open("myDoc.html"))

# Construct soup from a web document
# Remember that urlopen() does not add "http://"!
soup3 = BeautifulSoup(urlopen("http://www.networksciencelab.com/"))
```

The second optional argument to the object constructor is the markup parser —a Python component that is in charge of extracting HTML tags and entities. BeautifulSoup comes with four preinstalled parsers:

- "html.parser" (default, very fast, not very lenient; used for "simple" HTML documents)

- "lxml" (very fast, lenient)

- "xml" (for XML files only)

- "html5lib" (very slow, extremely lenient; used for HTML documents with complicated structure, or for all HTML documents if the parsing speed is not an issue)

When the soup is ready, you can pretty print the original markup document with the function soup.prettify().

The function soup.get_text() returns the text part of the markup document with all tags removed. Use this function to convert markup to plain text when it's the plain text you're interested in.

```
htmlString = '''
  <HTML>
  <HEAD><TITLE>My document</TITLE></HEAD>
  <BODY>Main text.</BODY></HTML>
'''
soup = BeautifulSoup(htmlString)
soup.get_text()
```

⇒ `'\nMy document\nMain text.\n'`

Often markup tags are used to locate certain file fragments. For example, you might be interested in the first row of the first table. Plain text alone is not helpful in getting there, but tags are, especially if they have class or id attributes.

BeautifulSoup uses a consistent approach to all vertical and horizontal relations between tags. The relations are expressed as attributes of the tag objects and resemble a file system hierarchy. The soup title, soup.title, is the soup object attribute. The value of the name object of the title's parent element is soup.title.parent.name.string, and the first cell in the first row of the first table is probably soup.body.table.tr.td.

Any tag t has a name t.name, a string value (t.string with the original content and a list of t.stripped_strings with removed whitespaces), the parent t.parent, the next t.next and the previous t.prev tags, and zero or more children t.children (tags within tags).

BeautifulSoup provides access to HTML tag attributes through a Python dictionary interface. If the object t represents a hyperlink (such as <a href="foobar.html">, then the string value of the destination of the hyperlink is t["href"].string. Note that HTML tags are case-insensitive.

Perhaps the most useful soup functions are soup.find() and soup.find_all(), which find the first instance or all instances of a certain tag. Here's how to find things:

- All instances of the tag <H2>:

```
level2headers = soup.find_all("H2")
```

- All bold or italic formats:

```
formats = soup.find_all(["i", "b", "em", "strong"])
```

- All tags that have a certain attribute (for example, id="link3"):

```
soup.find(id="link3")
```

- All hyperlinks and also the destination URL of the first link, using either the dictionary notation or the tag.get() function:

```
links = soup.find_all("a")
firstLink = links[0]["href"]
# Or:
firstLink = links[0].get("href")
```

By the way, both expressions in the last example fail if the attribute is not present. You must use the tag.has_attr() function to check the presence of an attribute before you extract it. The following expression combines BeautifulSoup and list comprehension to extract all links and their respective URLs and labels (useful for recursive web crawling):

```
with urlopen("http://www.networksciencelab.com/") as doc:
  soup = BeautifulSoup(doc)

links = [(link.string, link["href"])
  for link in soup.find_all("a")
  if link.has_attr("href")]
```

The value of links is a list of tuples:

```
[('Network Science Workshop',
 'http://www.slideshare.net/DmitryZinoviev/workshop-20212296'),
 «...»,('Academia.edu',
 'https://suffolk.academia.edu/DmitryZinoviev'),  ('ResearchGate',
 'https://www.researchgate.net/profile/Dmitry_Zinoviev')]
```

The versatility of HTML/XML is its strength, but this versatility is also its curse, especially when it comes to tabular data. Fortunately, you can store tabular data in rigid but easy-to-process CSV files, which you'll look at in the next unit.

Unit 14

Handling CSV Files

CSV is a structured text file format used to store and move tabular or nearly tabular data. It dates back to 1972 and is a format of choice for Microsoft Excel, Apache OpenOffice Calc, and other spreadsheet software. Data.gov,[1] a U.S. government website that provides access to publicly available data, alone provides 12,550 data sets in the CSV format.

A CSV file consists of columns representing variables and rows representing records. (Data scientists with a statistical background often call them observations.) The fields in a record are typically separated by commas, but other delimiters, such as tabs (tab-separated values [TSV]), colons, semicolons, and vertical bars, are also common. Stick to commas when you write your own files, but be prepared to face other separators in files written by those who don't follow this advice.

Keep in mind that sometimes what looks like a delimiter is not a delimiter at all. To allow delimiter-like characters within a field as a part of the variable value (as in ...,"Hello, world",...), enclose the fields in quote characters.

For convenience, the Python module csv provides a CSV reader and a CSV writer. Both objects take a previously opened text file handle as the first parameter (in the example, the file is opened with the newline='' option to avoid the need to strip the lines). You may provide the delimiter and the quote character, if needed, through the optional parameters delimiter and quotechar. Other optional parameters control the escape character, the line terminator, and so on.

```
with open("somefile.csv", newline='') as infile:
    reader = csv.reader(infile, delimiter=',', quotechar='"')
```

The first record of a CSV file often contains column headers and may be treated differently from the rest of the file. This is not a feature of the CSV format itself, but simply a common practice.

A CSV reader provides an iterator interface for use in a for loop. The iterator returns the next record as a list of string fields. The reader doesn't convert the fields to any numeric data type (it's still our job!) and doesn't strip them

---

1.　catalog.data.gov/dataset?res_format=CSV

of the leading whitespaces, unless instructed by passing the optional parameter skipinitialspace=True.

If the size of the CSV file is not known and is potentially large, you don't want to read all records at once. Instead, use incremental, iterative, row-by-row processing: read a row, process the row, discard the row, and then get another one.

A CSV writer provides the functions writerow() and writerows(). writerow() writes a sequence of strings or numbers into the file as one record. The numbers are converted to strings, so you have one less thing to worry about. In a similar spirit, writerows() writes a list of sequences of strings or numbers into the file as a collection of records.

In the following example, we'll use the csv module to extract the "Answer.Age" column from a CSV file. We'll assume that the index of the column is not known, but that the column definitely exists. Once we get the numbers, we'll know the mean and the standard deviation of the age variable with some little help from the module statistics.

First, open the file and read the data:

```
with open("demographics.csv", newline='') as infile:
  data = list(csv.reader(infile))
```

Examine data[0], which is the first record in the file. It must contain the column header of interest:

```
ageIndex = data[0].index("Answer.Age")
```

Finally, access the field of interest in the remaining records and calculate and display the statistics:

```
ages = [int(row[ageIndex]) for row in data[1:]]
print(statistics.mean(ages), statistics.stdev(ages))
```

The modules csv and statistics are low-end, "quick and dirty" tools. Later, in Chapter 6, *Working with Data Series and Frames*, on page 83, you'll look at how to use pandas data frames for a project that goes beyond the trivial exploration of a few columns.

Unit 15

Reading JSON Files

JSON is a lightweight data interchange format. Unlike pickle (mentioned earlier on page 27), JSON is language-independent but more restricted in terms of data representation.

JSON: Who Cares?

 Many popular websites, such as Twitter,[2] Facebook,[3] and Yahoo! Weather,[4] provide APIs that use JSON as the data interchange format.

JSON supports the following data types:

- Atomic data types—strings, numbers, true, false, null

- Arrays—an array corresponds to a Python list; it's enclosed in square brackets []; the items in an array don't have to be of the same data type:

    [1, 3.14, "a string", true, null]

- Objects—an object corresponds to a Python dictionary; it is enclosed in curly braces {}; every item consists of a key and a value, separated by a colon:

    {"age" : 37, "gender" : "male", "married" : true}

- Any recursive combinations of arrays, objects, and atomic data types (arrays of objects, objects with arrays as item values, and so on)

Unfortunately, some Python data types and structures, such as sets and complex numbers, cannot be stored in JSON files. Therefore, you need to convert them to representable data types before exporting to JSON. You can store a complex number as an array of two double numbers and a set as an array of items.

Storing complex data into a JSON file is called *serialization*. The opposite operation is called *deserialization*. Python handles JSON serialization and deserialization via the functions in the module json.

---

2. dev.twitter.com/overview/documentation

3. developers.facebook.com

4. developer.yahoo.com/weather/

The function dump() exports ("dumps") a representable Python object to a previously opened text file. The function dumps() exports a representable Python object to a text string (for the purpose of pretty printing or interprocess communications). Both functions are responsible for serialization.

The Value of Pickling

When you save data to a JSON file, the values of your variables are saved; after loading back, the values become independent. When you pickle the same data, the references to the original variables are saved; after loading back, all references to the same variable keep referencing the same variable.

The function loads() converts a valid JSON string into a Python object (it "loads" the object into Python). This conversion is always possible. In the same spirit, the function load() converts the content of a previously opened text file into one Python object. It is an error to store more than one object in a JSON file, but if an existing file still contains more than one object, you can read it as text, convert the text into an array of objects (by adding square brackets around the text and comma separators between the individual objects), and use loads() to deserialize the text to a list of objects.

The following code fragment subjects an arbitrary (but serializable) object to a sequence of serializations and deserializations:

```
object = «some serializable object»
# Save an object to a file
with open("data.json", "w") as out_json:
  json.dump(object, out_json, indent=None, sort_keys=False)
# Load an object from a file
with open("data.json") as in_json:
  object1 = json.load(in_json)
# Serialize an object to a string
json_string = json.dumps(object1)
# Parse a string as JSON
object2 = json.loads(json_string)
```

Tadaaam! Despite four painful conversions, object, object1, and object2 still have the same value.

Generally, use JSON representation to store final processing results when you anticipate that the results may be further processed by or imported into another program.

Unit 16

Processing Texts in Natural Languages

As a rule of thumb, somewhere around 80% of all potentially usable data is unstructured—which includes audio, video, images (all of them are beyond the scope of this book), and texts written in natural languages.[5] A text in a natural language has no tags, no delimiters, and no data types, but it still may be a rich source of information. We may want to know if (and how often) certain words are used in the text (*word and sentence tokenization*), what kind of text it is (*text classification*), whether it conveys a positive or negative message (*sentiment analysis*), who or what is mentioned in the text (*entity extraction*), and so on. We can read and process a text or two with our own eyes, but massive text analysis calls for automated natural language processing (NLP).

A lot of NLP functionality is implemented in the Python module nltk (Natural Language Toolkit). The module is organized around corpora (collections of words and expressions), functions, and algorithms.

NLTK Corpora

A corpus is a structured or unstructured collection of words or expressions. All NLTK corpora are stored in the module nltk.corpus. Some examples follow:

- gutenberg—contains eighteen English texts from the Gutenberg Project, such as *Moby Dick* and the Bible.

- names—a list of 8,000 male and female names.

- words—a list of 235,000 most frequently used English words and forms.

- stopwords—a list of stop words (the most frequently used words) in fourteen languages. The English list is in stopwords.words("english"). Stop words are usually eliminated from the text for most analyses types because they usually don't add anything to our understanding of texts.

---

5. www.informationweek.com/software/information-management/structure-models-and-meaning/d/d-id/1030187

- cmudict—a pronunciation dictionary composed at Carnegie Mellon University (hence the name), with over 134,000 entries. Each entry in cmudict.entries() is a tuple of a word and a list of syllables. The same word may have several different pronunciations. You can use this corpus to identify homophones ("soundalikes").

The object nltk.corpus.wordnet is an interface to another corpus—an online semantic word network WordNet (Internet access is required). The network is a collection of *synsets* (synonym sets)—words tagged with a part-of-speech marker and a sequential number:

```
wn = nltk.corpus.wordnet # The corpus reader
wn.synsets("cat")
```

⇒ **[Synset('cat.n.01'), Synset('guy.n.01'), «more synsets»]**

For each synset, you can look up its definition, which may be quite unexpected:

```
wn.synset("cat.n.01").definition()
wn.synset("cat.n.02").definition()
```

⇒ **'feline mammal usually having thick soft fur «...»'**
⇒ **'an informal term for a youth or man'**

A synset may have hypernyms (less specific synsets) and hyponyms (more specific synsets), which make synsets look like OOP classes with subclasses and superclasses.

```
wn.synset("cat.n.01").hypernyms()
wn.synset("cat.n.01").hyponyms()
```

⇒ **[Synset('feline.n.01')]**
⇒ **[Synset('domestic_cat.n.01'), Synset('wildcat.n.03')]**

Finally, you can use WordNet to calculate semantic similarity between two synsets. The similarity is a double number in the range [0...1]. If the similarity is 0, the synsets are unrelated; if it is 1, the synsets are full synonyms.

```
x = wn.synset("cat.n.01")
y = wn.synset("lynx.n.01")
x.path_similarity(y)
```

⇒ **0.04**

So, how close are two arbitrary words? Let's have a look at all synsets for "dog" and "cat" and find the definitions of the most semantically close of them:

```
[simxy.definition() for simxy in max(
  (x.path_similarity(y), x, y)
    for x in wn.synsets('cat')
    for y in wn.synsets('dog')
    if x.path_similarity(y) # Ensure the synsets are related at all
  )[1:]]
```

⇒ `['an informal term for a youth or man', 'informal term for a man']`

Surprise!

In addition to using the standard corpora, you can create your own corpora through the PlaintextCorpusReader. The reader looks for the files in the root directory that match the glob pattern.

```
myCorpus = nltk.corpus.PlaintextCorpusReader(root, glob)
```

The function fileids() returns the list of files included in the newly minted corpus. The function raw() returns the original "raw" text in the corpus. The function sents() returns the list of all sentences. The function words() returns the list of all words. You'll find out in the next section how the magic of converting raw text into sentences and words happens.

```
myCorpus.fileids()
myCorpus.raw()
myCorpus.sents()
myCorpus.words()
```

Use the latter function (described on page 42) in conjunction with a Counter object (described on page 17) to calculate word frequencies and identify the most frequently used words.

NLTK Is a Hollow Module

When you install the module NLTK, you actually install only the classes—but not the corpora. The corpora are considered too large to be included in the distribution. When you import the module for the first time, remember to call the function download() (an Internet connection is required) and install the missing parts, depending on your needs.

Normalization

Normalization is the procedure that prepares a text in a natural language for further processing. It typically involves the following steps (more or less in this order):

1. Tokenization (breaking the text into words). NLTK provides two simple and two more advanced tokenizers. The sentence tokenizer returns a list of sentences as strings. All other tokenizers return a list of words:

   - word_tokenize(text)—word tokenizer

   - sent_tokenize(text)—sentence tokenizer

   - regexp_tokenize(text, re)—regular expression-based tokenizer; parameter re is a regular expression that describes a valid word

   Depending on the quality of the tokenizer and the punctuational structure of the sentence, some "words" may contain non-alphabetic characters. For the tasks that heavily depend on punctuation analysis, such as sentiment analysis through emoticons, you need an advanced WordPunctTokenizer. Compare how WordPunctTokenizer.tokenize() and word_tokenize() parse the same text:

   ```
   from nltk.tokenize import WordPunctTokenizer
   word_punct = WordPunctTokenizer()
   text = "}Help! :))) :[ ..... :D{"
   word_punct.tokenize(text)
   ```

   ⇒ ["}", "Help", "!", ":)))", ":[", ".....", ":", "D", "{"]

   ```
   nltk.word_tokenize(text)
   ```

   ⇒ ["}", "Help", "!", ":", ")", ")", ")", ":", "[", "...",
   ⇒   "..", ":", "D", "{"]

2. Conversion of the words to all same-case characters (all uppercase or lowercase).

3. Elimination of stop words. Use the corpus stopwords and additional application-specific stop word lists as the reference. Remember that the words in stopwords are in lowercase. If you look up "THE" (definitely a stop word) in the corpus, it won't be there.

4. Stemming (conversion of word forms to their stems). NLTK supplies two basic stemmers: a less aggressive Porter stemmer and a more aggressive Lancaster stemmer. Due to its aggressive stemming rules, the Lancaster stemmer produces more homonymous stems. Both stemmers have the function stem(word) that returns the alleged stem of word:

```
pstemmer = nltk.PorterStemmer()
pstemmer.stem("wonderful")
```

⇒ **'wonder'**

```
lstemmer = nltk.LancasterStemmer()
lstemmer.stem("wonderful")
```

⇒ **'wond'**

Apply either stemmer only to single words, not to complete phrases. That's how they work!

5. Lemmatization—a slower and more conservative stemming mechanism. The WordNetLemmatizer looks up calculated stems in WordNet and accepts them only if they exist as words or forms. (Internet access is required to use the lemmatizer.) The function lemmatize(word) returns the lemma of word.

```
lemmatizer = nltk.WordNetLemmatizer()
lemmatizer.lemmatize("wonderful")
```

⇒ **'wonderful'**

Though technically not a part of the normalization sequence, the part-of-speech tagging (POS tagging) is nonetheless an important step in text preprocessing. The function nltk.pos_tag(text) assigns a part-of-speech tag to every word in the text, which is given as a list of words. The return value is a list of tuples, where the first element of a tuple is the original word and the second element is a tag.

```
nltk.pos_tag(["beautiful", "world"])
# An adjective and a noun
```

⇒ **[('beautiful', 'JJ'), ('world', 'NN')]**

To put everything together, let's display the ten most frequently used non-stop word stems in the file index.html. (Note the use of BeautifulSoup previously introduced on page 30!)

```
from bs4 import BeautifulSoup
from collections import Counter
from nltk.corpus import stopwords
from nltk import LancasterStemmer

# Create a new stemmer
ls = nltk.LancasterStemmer()

# Read the file and cook a soup
with open("index.html") as infile:
  soup = BeautifulSoup(infile)

# Extract and tokenize the text
```

```
words = nltk.word_tokenize(soup.text)
# Convert to lowercase
words = [w.lower() for w in words]

# Eliminate stop words and stem the rest of the words
words = [ls.stem(w) for w in text if w not in
  stopwords.words("english") and w.isalnum()]

# Tally the words
freqs = Counter(words)
print(freqs.most_common(10))
```

Think of this code fragment as the first step toward topic extraction.

Other Text-Processing Procedures

A lengthy discussion of other advanced NLP procedures is outside of the scope of this book, but here's a brief rundown of the options to pique your interest:

- Segmentation—recognition of "word" boundaries in a text that has no syntactic word boundaries (in a Chinese text, for example). You can apply segmentation to any character or numeric sequences (for example, to a sequence of purchases or DNA fragments).

- Text classification—assigning a text to one of the preset categories, based on predefined criteria. A special case of text classification is sentiment analysis, which is typically based on the analysis of frequencies of emotionally charged words.

- Entity extraction—detection of words or phrases with predetermined properties, usually referring to entities, such as persons, geographical locations, companies, products, and brands.

- Latent semantic indexing—identification of patterns in the relationships between the terms and concepts contained in an unstructured collection of text, using singular value decomposition (SVD). Incidentally, SVD is also known as principal component analysis (PCA) in statistics.

Your Turn

At this point, you know how to extract valuable data from an existing HTML, XML, CSV, or JSON file, or even from plain text. You understand HTML and XML tags and their structure, and you can separate tags from data and normalize words (at least to some extent). There are a lot of powerful projects that literally require just that—and some patience. Let's practice!

Broken Link Detector[*]

Write a program that, given a URL of a web page, reports the names and destinations of broken links in the page. For the purpose of this exercise, a link is broken if an attempt to open it with urllib.request.urlopen() fails.

Wikipedia Miner[**]

MediaWiki (a Wikimedia project[6]) provides a JSON-based API that enables programmable access to Wikipedia data and metadata. Write a program that reports ten most frequently used stems in the Wikipedia page titled "Data science."

Implementation hints:

- Use HTTP, not HTTPS.

- Read the "simple example" at the MediaWiki site and use it as the foundation of your program.

- First, get the page ID by title, then get the page by its ID.

- Visually explore the JSON data, especially the keys at different levels of hierarchy: at the time of writing, the answer is six levels deep!

Music Genre Classifier[***]

Write a program that uses Wikipedia to calculate semantic similarity between different rock/pop music genres. Start with the list of major music groups by genre[7] (note that the list is hierarchical and contains subcategories!). Recursively process the list and its descendants until all relevant groups are found (you may want to restrict your exploration to select subcategories, such as British rock groups, to save time and traffic). For each discovered group, extract the genres, if possible. Use the Jaccard similarity index[8] as a measure of semantic similarity: for each pair of genres A and B, $J(A,B)=|A \cap B| / |A \cup B|=|C|/(|A|+|B|-|C|)$, where $|A|$

---

6. www.mediawiki.org/wiki/API:Main_page
7. en.wikipedia.org/wiki/Category:Rock_music_groups_by_genre
8. en.wikipedia.org/wiki/Jaccard_index

and $|B|$ are the number of groups that list A or B as their genre, respectively, and $|C|$ is the number of groups that list both A and B. Pickle the results for future use: you don't want to run this program more than once!

By the way, how many genres are out there and what are the most strongly related genres?

Which are the goddesses?...The tenth is Vor, who is so wise and searching that nothing can be concealed from her.

  Snorri Sturluson, Icelandic historian, poet, and politician

## CHAPTER 4

Working with Databases

You study (or practice) *data* science. (Check!) You import raw data from disk files into Python *data* structures. (Check!) But all good things come in threes, and here's another *data* chapter: *data*bases are where you will store your data in the long run.

Databases are important components of the data analysis pipeline:

- Input data is often provided in the form of database tables. You must retrieve it from the database for further processing.

- Databases provide highly optimized, fast, non-volatile storage that you can use for storing raw data and intermediate and final results, even if the original raw data was not stored in a database.

- Databases provide highly optimized data transformations: sorting, selection, joining. If the raw data or the intermediate results are already in a database, you can use the database not just for storage, but also for aggregation.

In this chapter, you'll explore how to set up, configure, populate, and query MySQL and MongoDB—one of the most popular relational databases and the most popular document store (or NoSQL database), respectively. Though most likely you'll use these databases as preconfigured and prepopulated data sources, understanding the rich inner world of the database engine not only makes you a better programmer, but it also lays a solid foundation for introducing pandas in the future (on page 83).

Unit 17

Setting Up a MySQL Database

A *relational database* is a collection of permanently stored and possibly sorted and indexed tables. Relational databases are excellent for storing tabular data (such as data found in CSV files), where one table represents a variable type, the columns of the table represent variables, and the rows represent observations, or records.

You don't need Python to operate a database; however, you must know Structured Query Language (SQL) or its specific implementation, such as MySQL, to access a relational database either from its command line or from a Python application.

To interact with a running MySQL database server from the command line, you need a MySQL client, such as mysql. All MySQL commands are case-insensitive and must end with a semicolon.

To start a new database project, use mysql as the database administrator (these operations are executed only once):

1. Start mysql on the shell command line:

   ```
   c:\myProject> mysql -u root -p
   Enter password:
   Welcome to the MySQL monitor.  Commands end with ; or \g.
   «More mysql output»
   mysql>
   ```

   Enter all further instructions at the mysql command-line prompt.

2. Create a new database user ("dsuser") and password ("badpassw0rd"):

   ```
   CREATE USER 'dsuser'@'localhost' IDENTIFIED BY 'badpassw0rd';
   ```

3. Create a new database for the project ("dsdb"):

   ```
   CREATE DATABASE dsdb;
   ```

4. Grant the new user access to the new database:

   ```
   GRANT ALL ON dsdb.* TO 'dsuser'@'localhost';
   ```

Now, it's time to create a new table in an existing database. Use the same mysql client, but log in as a regular database user:

```
c:\myProject> mysql -u dsuser -p dsdb
Enter password:
Welcome to the MySQL monitor.  Commands end with ; or \g.
«More mysql output»
mysql>
```

Typically a table is created once and accessed many times. You can later change the table's properties to accommodate your project needs. The command CREATE TABLE, followed by the new table name and a list of columns, creates a new table. For each column, define its name and data type (in this order). The most common MySQL data types are TINYINT, SMALLINT, INT, FLOAT, DOUBLE, CHAR, VARCHAR, TINYTEXT, TEXT, DATE, TIME, DATETIME, and TIMESTAMP.

The following command creates the table employee with the columns empname (text of variable length), salary (floating point number), and hired (date). Each record in the table describes one employee.

```
USE dsdb;
CREATE TABLE employee (empname TINYTEXT, salary FLOAT, hired DATE);
```

⇒ **Query OK, 0 rows affected (0.17 sec)**

When you don't need a table anymore, you can drop it from the database.

```
DROP TABLE employee;
```

⇒ **Query OK, 0 rows affected (0.05 sec)**

The DROP command is short, elegant, and bitterly irreversible, like spilling your milk. Think twice before you drop anything!

Database Schema

 A *database schema* is the structure of the database that describes all tables, columns, data types, indexes, constraints, and relations between different tables. A schema is a hole in the donut: it's what's left of a database after all data is deleted from all tables.

Though not required by the language standard, you should always add an autogenerated primary key and auto-updated last modification timestamp to each record (as long as storage space permits). The primary key enables unique record identification and speeds up searches. The last modification timestamp adds a sense of history, and the NOT NULL keyword enforces that the marked columns actually have non-garbage values:

```
CREATE TABLE employee (id INT PRIMARY KEY AUTO_INCREMENT,
  updated TIMESTAMP, empname TINYTEXT NOT NULL, salary FLOAT NOT NULL,
  hired DATE);
```

If you want to use a column (variable) for sorting, searching, or joining, add an index to that column, too:

```
ALTER TABLE employee ADD INDEX(hired);
```

⇒ **Query OK, 0 rows affected (0.22 sec)**
⇒ **Records: 0 Duplicates: 0 Warnings: 0**

Note that indexes dramatically improve query times, but also substantially increase insertion and deletion times. Indexes should be created only after the main bulk of data is inserted into the table. If a new batch of data needs to be inserted, first remove the existing indexes:

```
DROP INDEX hired ON employee;
```

You can then insert the data and add the indexes back.

If all the values in a column are unique (such as employee ID numbers or names), add a UNIQUE constraint to that column. If the column data type has a variable width (such as VARCHAR, TINYTEXT, or TEXT), you must specify how much of each entry in the column must be unique:

```
ALTER TABLE employee ADD UNIQUE(empname(255));
```

The primary key always has a value (it is NOT NULL), it's always an INDEX, and it's UNIQUE.

Unit 18

Using a MySQL Database: Command Line

MySQL supports five basic database operations: insertion, deletion, mutation, selection, and join. They are used to populate database tables and modify and retrieve the existing data. These operations would normally originate in your data analysis program, but to get the sense of them, we will first practice them at the mysql command-line prompt.

Insertion

First things first. We'll insert a new record into a table, and then another one, and another one, until the table has all observations:

```
INSERT INTO employee VALUES(NULL,NULL,"John Smith",35000,NOW());
```

⇒ **Query OK, 1 row affected, 1 warning (0.18 sec)**

The first two NULLs are placeholder values of the index and the timestamp. The server calculates them automatically. The function NOW() returns the current date and time, but only the "date" part is used to populate the record. Note that the query produced a warning, and the reason for it is the latter truncation. Let's look at the verbal descriptions and codes of the most recent warning(s) and error(s):

```
SHOW WARNINGS;
```

⇒ `+-------+------+--------------------------------------------+`
⇒ `| Level | Code | Message                                    |`
⇒ `+-------+------+--------------------------------------------+`
⇒ `| Note  | 1265 | Data truncated for column 'hired' at row 1 |`
⇒ `+-------+------+--------------------------------------------+`
⇒ **1 row in set (0.00 sec)**

If an insertion operation violates the UNIQUE constraint, the server aborts it unless you specify the IGNORE keyword, in which case the insertion fails:

```
INSERT INTO employee VALUES(NULL,NULL,"John Smith",35000,NOW());
```

⇒ **ERROR 1062 (23000): Duplicate entry 'John Smith' for key 'empname'**

```
INSERT IGNORE INTO employee VALUES(NULL,NULL,"John Smith",35000,NOW());
```

⇒ **Query OK, 0 rows affected, 1 warning (0.14 sec)**

You could insert more rows by hand, but the preferred way is to let Python do the rest of the insertions.

Deletion

Deletion removes from the table all the records that match the search criterion. If you don't specify the search criterion, the server will remove all records:

```
-- Remove John Smith if he is low-paid
DELETE FROM employee WHERE salary<11000 AND empname="John Smith";
-- Remove everyone
DELETE FROM employee;
```

If you want to remove only a particular record, use its unique primary key or any other unique identifying condition:

```
DELETE FROM employee WHERE id=387513;
```

Remember that deletion is irreversible!

Mutation

Mutation updates the values of specified columns in the records that match the search criterion. If you don't specify the search criterion, the operation will affect all records:

```
-- Reset all recent hires' salary
UPDATE employee SET salary=35000 WHERE hired=CURDATE();
-- Increase John Smith's salary again
UPDATE employee SET salary=salary+1000 WHERE empname="John Smith";
```

```
Query OK, 1 row affected (0.06 sec)
Rows matched: 1  Changed: 1  Warnings: 0
```

And you've guessed it right: mutation is irreversible, too. Just like deletion, it is a destructive operation.

Selection

Selection selects all requested columns from all records that match the search criterion. If you don't specify the search criterion, you'll get all records, which may be way more than you want:

```
SELECT empname,salary FROM employee WHERE empname="John Smith";
```

```
+------------+--------+
| empname    | salary |
+------------+--------+
| John Smith |  36000 |
+------------+--------+
1 row in set (0.00 sec)
```

```
SELECT empname,salary FROM employee;
```

```
⇒ +--------------+--------+
⇒ | empname      | salary |
⇒ +--------------+--------+
⇒ | John Smith   |  36000 |
⇒ | Jane Doe     |  75000 |
⇒ | Abe Lincoln  |   0.01 |
⇒ | Anon I. Muss |  14000 |
⇒ +--------------+--------+
⇒ 4 rows in set (0.00 sec)
```

You can enhance selection by sorting, grouping, aggregating, and filtering the results. To sort the results, use the ORDER BY modifier (sorting by multiple columns in either DESCending or ASCending order is possible):

```
SELECT * FROM employee WHERE hired>='2000-01-01' ORDER BY salary DESC;
```

```
⇒ +----+---------------------+--------------+--------+------------+
⇒ | id | updated             | empname      | salary | hired      |
⇒ +----+---------------------+--------------+--------+------------+
⇒ |  4 | 2016-01-09 17:35:11 | Jane Doe     |  75000 | 2011-11-11 |
⇒ |  1 | 2016-01-09 17:31:29 | John Smith   |  36000 | 2016-01-09 |
⇒ |  6 | 2016-01-09 17:55:24 | Anon I. Muss |  14000 | 2011-01-01 |
⇒ +----+---------------------+--------------+--------+------------+
⇒ 3 rows in set (0.01 sec)
```

To group and aggregate the results, use the GROUP BY modifier and an aggregation function, such as COUNT(), MIN(), MAX(), SUM(), or AVG():

```
SELECT (hired>'2001-01-01') AS Recent,AVG(salary)
  FROM employee
  GROUP BY (hired>'2001-01-01');
```

```
⇒ +--------+---------------------+
⇒ | Recent | AVG(salary)         |
⇒ +--------+---------------------+
⇒ |      0 | 0.009999999776482582 |
⇒ |      1 |    41666.666666666664 |
⇒ +--------+---------------------+
⇒ 2 rows in set (0.00 sec)
```

The latter statement calculates and reports the average salary of each group of employees based on whether they were hired before or after 01/01/2001, as well as the hiring range itself.

The keywords WHERE and HAVING filter the selection results; the server executes WHERE before grouping and HAVING after grouping.

```
SELECT AVG(salary),MIN(hired),MAX(hired) FROM employee
  GROUP BY YEAR(hired)
```

```
    HAVING MIN(hired)>'2001-01-01';
```

```
⇒ +-------------+------------+------------+
⇒ | AVG(salary) | MIN(hired) | MAX(hired) |
⇒ +-------------+------------+------------+
⇒ |       44500 | 2011-01-01 | 2011-11-11 |
⇒ |       36000 | 2016-01-09 | 2016-01-09 |
⇒ +-------------+------------+------------+
⇒ 2 rows in set (0.00 sec)
```

This statement calculates and reports the average salary and the earliest and latest hiring dates for each group hired on the same year after 01/01/2001.

Join

The join operation combines the contents of two tables based on one or more columns. MySQL supports five types of joins: inner (with a flavor called straight join), left, right, outer, and natural. The latter can also be left or right. The inner join returns rows with at least one match in both tables. Left/right joins all rows from the left/right table, respectively, even if there is no match on the other side. Outer returns rows with a match in either table. If one table doesn't have a match, the server returns a NULL instead. A natural join behaves like outer, except that it implicitly involves all columns with the same names.

The following commands create a new table with employee positions, add an index to the column that will be used for joining, and extract employee names and positions from both tables (the syntax in the latter example is for an implicit inner join):

```
-- Prepare and populate another table
CREATE TABLE position (eid INT, description TEXT);
INSERT INTO position (eid,description) VALUES (6,'Imposter'),
  (1,'Accountant'),(4,'Programmer'),(5,'President');
ALTER TABLE position ADD INDEX(eid);
```

```
-- Fetch the joined data
SELECT employee.empname,position.description
  FROM employee,position WHERE employee.id=position.eid
  ORDER BY position.description;
```

```
⇒ +-------------+------------+
⇒ | empname     | description |
⇒ +-------------+------------+
⇒ | John Smith  | Accountant |
⇒ | Anon I. Muss | Imposter  |
⇒ | Abe Lincoln | President  |
⇒ | Jane Doe    | Programmer |
⇒ +-------------+------------+
⇒ 4 rows in set (0.00 sec)
```

Unit 19

Using a MySQL Database: pymysql

Python uses a database driver module to communicate with MySQL. Several database drivers, such as pymysql, are freely available. For this exercise, you'll use pymysql, which is a part of Anaconda. The driver, when activated, connects to the database server and then transforms Python function calls into database queries and, conversely, database results into Python data structures.

The function connect() requires the information about the database (its name), the whereabouts of the database server (the host and the port number), and the database user (name and password). If successfully connected, it returns the connection identifier. As the next step, create a database cursor associated with the connection:

```
conn = pymysql.connect(host="localhost", port=3306,
  user="dsuser", passwd="badpassw0rd", db="dsdb")
cur = conn.cursor()
```

The execute() function of the cursor submits a query for execution and returns the number of affected rows (zero, if the query is non-destructive). The query is simply a character string that you prepare based on what you learned in the previous unit. Unlike a command-line MySQL query, a pymysql query needs no terminating semicolon.

```
query = '''
SELECT employee.empname,position.description
  FROM employee,position WHERE employee.id=position.eid
  ORDER BY position.description
'''
n_rows = cur.execute(query)
```

If you submit a non-destructive query (such as SELECT), use the cursor function fetchall() to obtain all matching records. The function returns a generator that you can convert into a list of tuples of column fields:

```
results = list(cur.fetchall())
```

⇒ [('John Smith', 'Accountant'), ('Anon I. Muss', 'Imposter'),
⇒ ('Abe Lincoln', 'President'), ('Jane Doe', 'Programmer')]

If the query is destructive (such as UPDATE, DELETE, or INSERT), you must commit it. (Note that it's the connection, not the cursor, that provides the function commit().)

```
conn.commit()
```

If you don't commit a destructive query, the server will not modify the tables.

Relational databases have been around since 1974 (Ingres).[1] They have a venerable legacy and work great with normalized data—that is, the data that can naturally be split into tables, columns, and rows. Honestly, any data set can be normalized, but the price of normalizing can be prohibitively high (both in terms of normalization effort and eventual query performance). Certain types of data (text documents, images, audio and video clips, and irregular data structures in the first place) naturally resist normalization. Don't force them to fit the procrustean SQL-ean bed; rather, choose a NoSQL document store instead, which is introduced next.

---

1. quickbase.intuit.com/articles/timeline-of-database-history

Unit 20

Taming Document Stores: MongoDB

A *document store* (a NoSQL database) is a non-volatile collection of objects, often known as documents, with attributes. Many different implementations of document stores have been developed. In this unit, you'll look closely at one of them—MongoDB—and take a quick peek at its chief competitor, CouchDB.[2]

MongoDB is a non-relational database. One MongoDB server can support several unrelated databases. A database consists of one or more collections of documents. All documents in a collection have unique identifiers.

A Python MongoDB client is implemented in the Python module pymongo as an instance of the class MongoClient. You can create a client with no parameters (works for a typical local server installation), with the host name and port number of the server as the parameters, or with the Uniform Resource Identifier (URI) of the server as the parameter:

```
import pymongo as mongo
# Default initialization
client1 = mongo.MongoClient()
# Explicit host and port
client2 = mongo.MongoClient("localhost", 27017)
# Explicit host and port as a URI
client3 = mongo.MongoClient("mongodb://localhost:27017/")
```

Once the client establishes a connection to the database server, select the active database and then the active collection. You can use either the object-oriented ("dotted") or dictionary-style notation. If the selected database or collection do not exist, the server will create them at once:

```
# Two ways to create/select the active database
db = client1.dsdb
db = client1["dsdb"]

# Two ways to create/select the active collection
people = db.people
people = db["people"]
```

---

2. couchdb.apache.org

pymongo represents MongoDB documents as Python dictionaries. Each dictionary representing an object must have the _id key. If the key is absent, the server autogenerates it.

A collection object provides functions for inserting, searching, removing, updating, replacing, and aggregating documents in the collection, as well as for creating indexes.

The functions insert_one(doc) and insert_many(docs) insert a document or a list of documents into a collection. They return the objects InsertOneResult or Insert-ManyResult, respectively, which, in turn, provide the attributes inserted_id and inserted_ids. Use these attributes to discover the documents' keys if the documents have no explicit keys. If the _id key is specified, it won't change after insertion:

```
person1 = {"empname" : "John Smith", "dob" : "1957-12-24"}
person2 = {"_id" : "XVT162", "empname" : "Jane Doe", "dob" : "1964-05-16"}
person_id1 = people.insert_one(person1).inserted_id
```

⇒ **ObjectId('5691a8720f759d05092d311b')**

```
# Note the new "_id" field!
person1
```

⇒ **{'empname': 'John Smith', 'dob': '1957-12-24',**
⇒ **'_id': ObjectId('5691a8720f759d05092d311b')}**

```
person_id2 = people.insert_one(person2).inserted_id
```

⇒ **"XVT162"**

```
persons = [{"empname" : "Abe Lincoln", "dob" : "1809-02-12"},
           {"empname" : "Anon I. Muss"}]
result = people.insert_many(persons)
result.inserted_ids
```

⇒ **[ObjectId('5691a9900f759d05092d311c'),**
⇒ **ObjectId('5691a9900f759d05092d311d')]**

The functions find_one() and find() report one or many documents that optionally match certain properties. find_one() returns the document, and find() returns a cursor (a generator) that you can convert to a list with the list() function or use as an iterator in a for loop. If you pass a dictionary as the parameter to either of these functions, the functions report the documents whose values are equal to all dictionary values for the respective keys:

```
everyone = people.find()
list(everyone)
```

⇒ [{'empname': 'John Smith', 'dob': '1957-12-24',
⇒   '_id': ObjectId('5691a8720f759d05092d311b')},
⇒ {'empname': 'Jane Doe', 'dob': '1964-05-16', '_id': 'XVT162'},
⇒ {'empname': 'Abe Lincoln', 'dob': '1809-02-12',
⇒   '_id': ObjectId('5691a9900f759d05092d311c')},
⇒ {'empname': 'Anon I. Muss', '_id': ObjectId('5691a9900f759d05092d311d')}]

```
list(people.find({"dob" : "1957-12-24"}))
```

⇒ [{'empname': 'John Smith', 'dob': '1957-12-24',
⇒   '_id': ObjectId('5691a8720f759d05092d311b')}]

```
people.find_one()
```

⇒ [{'empname': 'John Smith', 'dob': '1957-12-24',
⇒   '_id': ObjectId('5691a8720f759d05092d311b')}]

```
people.find_one({"empname" : "Abe Lincoln"})
```

⇒ {'empname': 'Abe Lincoln', 'dob': '1809-02-12',
⇒ '_id': ObjectId('5691a9900f759d05092d311c')}

```
people.find_one({"_id" : "XVT162"})
```

⇒ {'empname': 'Jane Doe', 'dob': '1964-05-16', '_id': 'XVT162'}

Several grouping and sorting functions allow data aggregation and sorting. The function sort() sorts the results of the query. When you call it with no arguments, sort() sorts by the key _id in the ascending order. The function count() returns the number of documents in the query or in the entire collection:

```
people.count()
```

⇒ 4

```
people.find({"dob": "1957-12-24"}).count()
```

⇒ 1

```
people.find().sort("dob")
```

⇒ [{'empname': 'Anon I. Muss', '_id': ObjectId('5691a9900f759d05092d311d')},
⇒ {'empname': 'Abe Lincoln', 'dob': '1809-02-12',
⇒   '_id': ObjectId('5691a9900f759d05092d311c')},
⇒ {'empname': 'John Smith', 'dob': '1957-12-24',
⇒   '_id': ObjectId('5691a8720f759d05092d311b')},
⇒ {'empname': 'Jane Doe', 'dob': '1964-05-16', '_id': 'XVT162'}]

The functions delete_one(doc) and delete_many(docs) remove a document or documents identified by the dictionary doc from the collection. To remove all of the documents, but keep the collection, call delete_many({}) with an empty dictionary as the parameter:

```
result = people.delete_many({"dob" : "1957-12-24"})
result.deleted_count
```

⇒ **1**

CouchDB

Another popular NoSQL database is CouchDB. Unlike MongoDB, CouchDB favors availability over consistency. If CouchDB is replicated (runs on more than one computer), then all its users can always use it but do not necessarily observe the same documents. If MongoDB is replicated, then its users see exactly the same documents, but for some users the database may not be available at all. If you don't plan to replicate your database, the choice between CouchDB and MongoDB is purely aesthetic.

Your Turn

Managing databases is a major scientific field that is well beyond the scope of this book. Reading this chapter alone won't make you a seasoned database administrator or a versatile database programmer. But, now you can create a table or two, store data into them, and get the data back when you need it, and you can do it two ways: with or without SQL.

MySQL File Indexer[*]

Write a Python program that, for each word in a given file, records the word itself (not the stem!), its ordinal number in the file (starting from 1), and the part-of-speech marker in a MySQL database. Use NLTK WordPunct-Tokenizer (introduced on page 41) to recognize words. Assume that the words are short enough to fit in the TINYTEXT MySQL data type. Design the database schema, create all necessary tables, and play with them via the command-line interface before starting any Python coding.

MySQL to MongoDB Converter[**]

The MySQL statement DESCRIBE table_name reports the names, data types, constraints, default values, and so on of all columns in the table. Write a Python program that transfers all data from a MySQL table (designated by the user) to a MongoDB document. The program must not modify timestamps.

It is a capital mistake to theorize before one has data.

　　Sir Arthur Conan Doyle, British writer

## CHAPTER 5

Working with Tabular Numeric Data

Often raw data comes from all kinds of text documents. Quite often the text actually represents numbers. Excel and CSV spreadsheets and especially database tables may contain millions or billions of numerical records. Core Python is an excellent text-processing tool, but it sometimes fails to deliver adequate numeric performance. That's where numpy comes to the rescue.

NumPy—Numeric Python (imported as numpy)—is an interface to a family of efficient and parallelizable functions that implement high-performance numerical operations. The module numpy provides a new Python data structure —array—and a toolbox of array-specific functions, as well as support for random numbers, data aggregation, linear algebra, Fourier transform, and other goodies.

Bridge to Terabytia

If your program needs access to huge amounts of numerical data —terabytes and more—you can't avoid using the module h5py.[1] The module is a portal to the HDF5 binary data format that works with a lot of third-party software, such as IDL and MATLAB. h5py imitates familiar numpy and Python mechanisms, such as arrays and dictionaries. Once you know how to use numpy, you can go straight to h5py—but not in this book.

In this chapter, you'll learn how to create numpy arrays of different shapes and from different sources, reshape and slice arrays, add array indexes, and apply arithmetic, logic, and aggregation functions to some or all array elements.

---

1. www.h5py.org

Creating Arrays

numpy arrays are more compact and faster than native Python lists, especially in multidimensional cases. However, unlike lists, arrays are homogeneous: you cannot mix and match array items that belong to different data types.

There are several ways to create a numpy array. The function array() creates an array from array-like data. The data can be a list, a tuple, or another array. numpy infers the type of the array elements from the data, unless you explicitly pass the dtype parameter. numpy supports close to twenty data types, such as bool_, int64, uint64, float64, and <U32 (for Unicode strings).

When numpy creates an array, it doesn't copy the data from the source to the new array, but it links to it for efficiency reasons. This means that, by default, a numpy array is a view of its underlying data, not a copy of it. If the underlying data object changes, the array data changes, too. If this behavior is undesirable (which it always is, unless the amount of data to copy is prohibitively large), pass copy=True to the constructor.

Lists Are Arrays, and Arrays Are Arrays, Too

Contrary to their name, Python "lists" are actually implemented as arrays, not as lists. No storage is reserved for forward pointers, because no forward pointers are used. Large Python lists require only about 13% more storage than "real" numpy arrays. However, Python executes some simple built-in operations, such as sum(), five to ten times faster on lists than on arrays. Ask yourself if you really need any numpy-specific features before you start a numpy project!

Let's create our first array—a silly array of the first ten positive integer numbers:

```
import numpy as np
numbers = np.array(range(1, 11), copy=True)
```

⇒ `array([1, 2, 3, 4, 5, 6, 7, 8, 9, 10])`

The functions ones(), zeros(), and empty() construct arrays of all ones, all zeros, and all uninitialized entries, respectively. They then take a required shape parameter—a list or tuple of array dimensions.

```
ones = np.ones([2, 4], dtype=np.float64)
```

⇒ **array([[1., 1., 1., 1.],**
⇒ **[1., 1., 1., 1.]])**

```
zeros = np.zeros([2, 4], dtype=np.float64)
```

⇒ **array([[0., 0., 0., 0.],**
⇒ **[0., 0., 0., 0.]])**

```
empty = np.empty([2, 4], dtype=np.float64)
# The array content is not always zeros!
```

⇒ **array([[0., 0., 0., 0.],**
⇒ **[0., 0., 0., 0.]])**

numpy stores the number of dimensions, the shape, and the data type of an array in the attributes ndim, shape, and dtype.

```
ones.shape # The original shape, unless reshaped
```

⇒ **(2, 4)**

```
numbers.ndim # Same as len(numbers.shape)
```

⇒ **1**

```
zeros.dtype
```

⇒ **dtype('float64')**

The function eye(N, M=None, k=0, dtype=np.float) constructs an N×M *eye*-dentity matrix with ones on the kth diagonal and zeros elsewhere. Positive k denotes the diagonals above the main diagonal. When M is None (default), M=N.

```
eye = np.eye(3, k=1)
```

⇒ **array([[0., 1., 0.],**
⇒ **[0., 0., 1.],**
⇒ **[0., 0., 0.]])**

When you need to multiply several matrices, use an identity matrix as the initial value of the accumulator in the multiplication chain.

In addition to the good old built-in range(), numpy has its own, more efficient way of generating arrays of regularly spaced numbers: the function arange([start,] stop[, step,], dtype=None).

```
np_numbers = np.arange(2, 5, 0.25)
```

⇒ `array([ 2.  ,  2.25,  2.5 ,  2.75,  3.  ,  3.25,  3.5 ,  3.75,  4.  ,`
⇒ `       4.25,  4.5 ,  4.75])`

Just like with range(), the value of stop can be smaller than start—but then step must be negative, and the order of numbers in the array is decreasing.

numpy records the type of items at the time of array creation, but the type is not immutable: you can change it later by calling the astype(dtype, casting="unsafe", copy=True) function. In the case of type narrowing (converting to a more specific data type), some information may be lost. This is true about any narrowing, not just in numpy.

```
np_inumbers = np_numbers.astype(np.int)
```

⇒ `array([2, 2, 2, 2, 3, 3, 3, 3, 4, 4, 4, 4])`

Most numpy operations (such as transposing, which is discussed in the next unit on page 67) return a view, not a copy of the original array. To preserve original data, the function copy() creates a copy of an existing array. Any changes to the original array don't affect the copy, but if your array has one billion items, think twice before copying it.

```
np_inumbers_copy = np_inumbers.copy()
```

Let's now proceed to more advanced operations.

Unit 22

Transposing and Reshaping

Unlike the great monuments of the past, numpy arrays are not carved in stone. They can easily change their shape and orientation without being called opportunists. Let's build a one-dimensional array of some S&P stock symbols and twist it in every possible way:

```
# Some S&P stock symbols
sap = np.array(["MMM", "ABT", "ABBV", "ACN", "ACE", "ATVI", "ADBE", "ADT"])
```

⇒ array('MMM', 'ABT', 'ABBV', 'ACN', 'ACE', 'ATVI', 'ADBE', 'ADT'],
⇒   dtype='<U4')

The function reshape(d0, d1, ...) changes the shape of an existing array. The arguments define the new dimensions. The total number of items in the old and new shapes must be equal: the conservation law still holds in numpyland!

```
sap2d = sap.reshape(2, 4)
```

⇒ array([['MMM', 'ABT', 'ABBV', 'ACN'],
⇒   ['ACE', 'ATVI', 'ADBE', 'ADT']],
⇒   dtype='<U4')

```
sap3d = sap.reshape(2, 2, 2)
```

⇒ array([[['MMM', 'ABT'],
⇒   ['ABBV', 'ACN']],
⇒
⇒   [['ACE', 'ATVI'],
⇒   ['ADBE', 'ADT']]],
⇒   dtype='<U4')

To transpose an array, you don't even need to call a function: the value of the attribute T is the transposed view of the array (for a one-dimensional array, data.T==data; for a two-dimensional array, the rows and the columns are swapped).

```
sap2d.T
```

⇒ array([['MMM', 'ACE'],
⇒   ['ABT', 'ATVI'],
⇒   ['ABBV', 'ADBE'],
⇒   ['ACN', 'ADT']],
⇒   dtype='<U4')

Essentially, the attribute T shows us the matrix through a relabeling cross-hair: axis number 0 ("vertical") becomes axis number 1 ("horizontal"), and the other way around. The function swapaxes() is a more general version of the T. It transposes a multidimensional array by swapping any two axes that you pass as the parameters. Naturally, passing the axes 0 and 1 for a two-dimensional array simply transposes the array, just as before.

```
sap3d.swapaxes(1, 2)
```

```
⇒ array([[['MMM', 'ABBV'],
⇒         ['ABT', 'ACN']],
⇒
⇒        [['ACE', 'ADBE'],
⇒         ['ATVI', 'ADT']]],
⇒       dtype='<U4')
```

The function transpose() is even more general than swapaxes() (despite its name implying similarity to the T attribute). transpose() permutes some or all axes of a multidimensional array according to its parameter, which must be a tuple. In the following example, the first axis remains "vertical," but the other two axes are swapped.

```
sap3d.transpose((0, 2, 1))
```

```
⇒ array([[['MMM', 'ABBV'],
⇒         ['ABT', 'ACN']],
⇒
⇒        [['ACE', 'ADBE'],
⇒         ['ATVI', 'ADT']]],
⇒       dtype='<U4')
```

Incidentally, the result is the same as for swapaxes(1, 2)!

Unit 23

Indexing and Slicing

numpy arrays support the same indexing [i] and slicing [i:j] operations as Python lists. In addition, they implement Boolean indexing: you can use an array of Boolean values as an index, and the result of the selection is the array of items of the original array for which the Boolean index is True. Often the Boolean array is in turn a result of broadcasting. You can use Boolean indexing on the right-hand side (for selection) and on the left-hand side (for assignment).

Suppose your data sponsor told you that all data in the data set dirty is strictly non-negative. This means that any negative value is not a true value but an error, and you must replace it with something that makes more sense—say, with a zero. This operation is called *data cleaning*. To clean the dirty data, locate the offending values and substitute them with reasonable alternatives.

```
dirty = np.array([9, 4, 1, -0.01, -0.02, -0.001])
whos_dirty = dirty < 0 # Boolean array, to be used as Boolean index
```

⇒ **array([False, False, False, True, True, True], dtype=bool)**

```
dirty[whos_dirty] = 0 # Change all negative values to 0
```

⇒ **array([9, 4, 1, 0, 0, 0])**

You can combine several Boolean expressions with the operators | (logical or), & (logical and), and - (logical not). Which of the items in the following list are between -0.5 and 0.5? Ask numpy!

```
linear = np.arange(-1, 1.1, 0.2)
(linear <= 0.5) & (linear >= -0.5)
```

⇒ **array([False, False, False, True, True, True, True, True, False,**
⇒ **   False, False], dtype=bool)**

Boolean and "Boolean"

Relational operators (such as < and ==) have lower precedence than the bit-wise operators &, |, and ! that represent "Boolean" operators on numpy arrays. This is very confusing, because "normal" Python Boolean operators—or, and, and not—have lower precedence than the relational operators. You must enclose array comparisons in parentheses to ensure that numpy evaluates them first.

Another cool feature of numpy arrays is "smart" indexing and "smart" slicing, whereby an index is not a scalar but an array or list of indexes. The result of the selection is the array of items that are referenced in the index. Let's select the second, the third, and the last stock symbols from our S&P list. (That's "smart" indexing.)

```
sap[[1, 2, -1]]
```

```
⇒   array(['ABT', 'BBV', 'ADT'],
⇒         dtype='<U4')
```

Why not extract all rows in the middle column from the reshaped array? (That's "smart" slicing.) In fact, you can do it two ways:

```
sap2d[:, [1]]
```

```
⇒   array([['ABT'],
⇒          ['ATVI']],
⇒         dtype='<U4')
```

```
sap2d[:, 1]
```

```
⇒   array(['ABT', 'ATVI'],
⇒         dtype='<U4')
```

Python is famous for giving us many similar problem-solving tools and not forgiving us for choosing a wrong one. Compare the two selections shown earlier. The first selection is a two-dimensional matrix; the second one is a one-dimensional array. Depending on what you wanted to extract, one of them is wrong. Oops. Make sure you check that you've gotten what you wanted.

Unit 24

Broadcasting

numpy arrays eagerly engage in vectorized arithmetic operations with other arrays—as long as they're of the same shape. To add two arrays element-wise without numpy, you must use a for loop or list comprehension; with numpy, you simply add them up:

```
a = np.arange(4)
b = np.arange(1, 5)
a + b
```

⇒ **array([1, 3, 5, 7])**

Vectorized operations on arrays are known as broadcasting. Broadcasting along two dimensions is possible if they are equal (as above) or one of them is a scalar (as below):

```
a * 5
```

⇒ **array([0, 5, 10, 15])**

Be Fruitful or Multiply?

 The star operator (*) behaves differently in Python and numpy. The "core" Python expression seq * 5 replicates the list seq five times. The same numpy expression multiplies each element of array seq by five.

You can mix and match different arithmetic operations on arrays and scalars. Let's create a diagonal matrix and add some small (but not random) noise to it:

```
noise = np.eye(4) + 0.01 * np.ones((4, ))
```

⇒ **array([[1.01, 0.01, 0.01, 0.01],**
⇒ **   [0.01, 1.01, 0.01, 0.01],**
⇒ **   [0.01, 0.01, 1.01, 0.01],**
⇒ **   [0.01, 0.01, 0.01, 1.01]])**

But what if you want some small *and* random noise? We will seriously talk about random number generators later in Unit 47, *Doing Stats the Python Way*, on page 152, but here's a sneak preview:

```
noise = np.eye(4) + 0.01 * np.random.random([4, 4])
np.round(noise, 2)
```

⇒ **array([[1.01, 0. , 0.01, 0.],**
⇒ **   [0.01, 1.01, 0. , 0.01],**
⇒ **   [0. , 0. , 1. , 0.],**
⇒ **   [0. , 0. , 0.01, 1.]])**

Here we rounded the matrix with the *universal function* round()—all items in one function call! In Unit 25, *Demystifying Universal Functions*, on page 73, we'll become real *ufuncs* wizards.

By the way, if you run the previous example several times, you will get different results. That's because the random numbers are...random!

A more detailed and highly graphic study of real-world, noisy, sine wave–style signal generation awaits you in Unit 30, *Generating a Synthetic Sine Wave*, on page 80.

Unit 25

Demystifying Universal Functions

Vectorized universal functions, or *ufuncs*, are a functional counterpart of broadcasting. You can apply ufuncs to all array items at once in one function call. numpy provides a lot of ufuncs, and here are some of them:

- arithmetic: add(), multiply(), negative(), exp(), log(), sqrt()

- trigonometric: sin(), cos(), hypot()

- bitwise: bitwise_and(), left_shift()

- relational and logical: less(), logical_not(), equal()

- maximum() and minimum()

- functions for working with floating-point numbers: isinf(), isfinite(), floor(), isnan()

Let's say we recorded the stock prices for the eight sap symbols after and before the weekend of 01/10/2016 in a one-dimensional array called stocks:

```
stocks
```

```
array([ 140.49,    0.97,   40.68,   41.53,   55.7 ,   57.21,   98.2 ,
         99.19,  109.96,  111.47,   35.71,   36.27,   87.85,   89.11,
         30.22,   30.91])
```

We want to know which stock prices fell over the weekend. We'll first group the prices by symbols and put newer quotes after older quotes—by reshaping the original array into a 2×8 matrix:

```
stocks = stocks.reshape(8, 2).T
```

```
array([[ 140.49,   40.68,   55.7 ,   98.2 ,  109.96,   35.71,   87.85,
          30.22],
       [   0.97,   41.53,   57.21,   99.19,  111.47,   36.27,   89.11,
          30.91]])
```

Now we can apply the function greater() to both rows, perform a column-wise comparison, and find out the symbol of interest using Boolean indexing:

```
fall = np.greater(stocks[0], stocks[1])
```

⇒ **array([True, False, False, False, False, False, False, False], dtype=bool)**

```
sap[fall]
```

⇒ **array(['MMM'],**
⇒ **   dtype='<U4')**

Incidentally, MMM is a Ponzi scheme–based Russian company that has never been listed at any stock exchange. No wonder its stock is in decline.

In addition to "traditional" numbers, numpy fully supports the IEEE 754 floating-point standard and provides symbols for positive infinity (inf) and not-a-number (nan). They exist outside numpy as float("inf") and float("nan"). In accordance with the data scientific tradition, we will use nan as a placeholder for missing data (previously introduced on page 3).

The universal function isnan() is an excellent tool for locating the outcasts. And though replacing the missing data with a zero in the following example is probably a very bad idea, we did it before (on page 69), so let's do it again:

```
# Pretend the new MMM quote is missing
stocks[1, 0] = np.nan
np.isnan(stocks)
```

⇒ **array([[False, False, False, False, False, False, False, False],**
⇒ **   [True, False, False, False, False, False, False, False]], dtype=bool)**

```
# Repair the damage; it can't get worse than this
stocks[np.isnan(stocks)] = 0
```

⇒ **array([[140.49,   40.68,   55.7 ,   98.2 , 109.96,   35.71,   87.85,**
⇒ **   30.22],**
⇒ **   [0. ,   41.53,   57.21,   99.19, 111.47,   36.27,   89.11,**
⇒ **   30.91]])**

Universal functions expand the possibilities of Python arithmetic functions and relational operators. Conditional functions are Python logical operators on steroids.

Unit 26

Understanding Conditional Functions

The function where(c, a, b) is the numpy idea of the ternary operator if-else. It takes a Boolean array (c) and two other arrays (a and b) and returns array d[i]=a[i] if c[i] else b[i]. All three arrays must be of the same shape.

The functions any() and all() return True if any or all array elements are True, respectively.

The function nonzero() returns the indexes of all non-zero elements.

In Unit 25, *Demystifying Universal Functions*, on page 73, we recorded some S&P stock prices in an array sap. To find out which stock changed substantially (by more than $1.00 per share), let's replace "small" changes with zeros, locate the non-zero elements, and use their indexes as a "smart index" into the array of stock symbols:

```
changes = np.where(np.abs(stocks[1] - stocks[0]) > 1.00,
                   stocks[1] - stocks[0], 0)
```

⇒ **array([-139.52,   0. ,   1.51,   0. ,   1.51,   0. ,   1.26,   0.])**

```
sap[np.nonzero(changes)]
```

⇒ **array(['MMM', 'ABBV', 'ACE', 'ADBE'],**
⇒ **dtype='<U4')**

You could surely get the same answer using Boolean indexes alone:

```
sap[np.abs(stocks[1] - stocks[0]) > 1.00]
```

⇒ **array(['MMM', 'ABBV', 'ACE', 'ADBE'],**
⇒ **dtype='<U4')**

But it would not be so much fun!

Unit 27

Aggregating and Ordering Arrays

Data ordering and aggregation are at the core of data science. You start with large amounts of data and gradually distill them by binning, averaging, accumulating, and so on, until they hopefully boil down to a small, easily presentable, and easily interpretable set. numpy provides the functions mean(), sum(), std() (standard deviation), min(), and max() that return the respective aggregated measures of a numpy array.

Let's use a combination of broadcasting, aggregation functions, ufuncs, and Boolean indexes—almost our entire toolset!—to extract the stocks from Unit 25, *Demystifying Universal Functions*, on page 73, that changed either way by more than the average eight-stock portfolio:

```
sap[          np.abs(stocks[0] - stocks[1])
    > np.mean(np.abs(stocks[0] - stocks[1])))]
```

```
⇒  array(['MMM'],
⇒        dtype='<U4')
```

But, honestly, mixing positive and negative stock quote changes sounds like another horrible idea.

The functions cumsum(x) and cumprod(x) calculate cumulative sums and products: $cumsum_i = \Sigma_1^i x_i$ and $cumprod_i = \Pi_1^i x_i$. You can use them as poor man integrators of additive (simple interest payments) and multiplicative (compound interest payments) data. (Beware that if any array element is 0, its corresponding cumprod() element and all subsequent elements are 0, too.)

Let's compare simple and compound interest payments over 30 years with the interest rate of 3.75%—all in two lines of numpy code, plus (plotting) fees and taxes:

interest.py
```
# This is a partial listing
RATE = .0375
TERM = 30
simple =   (      RATE  * np.ones(TERM)).cumsum()
compound = ((1 + RATE) * np.ones(TERM)).cumprod() - 1
```

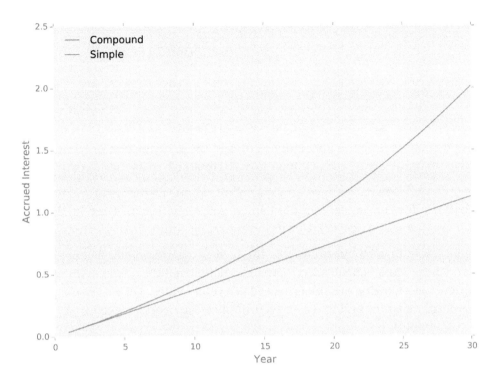

The function sort() is perhaps the most boring function in the module. It simply sorts an array in place (overwrites the original array order) and returns None. If the original array is precious to you, make a copy before sorting.

Unit 28

Treating Arrays as Sets

In some cases, the order of items in an array is less important than the array composition—whether a particular item is in the array or not, or what kind of items are in the array. numpy knows how to treat arrays as mathematical sets.

The function unique(x) returns an array of all unique elements of x. It's a great substitute for the Counter module (which you looked at in Unit 7, *Counting with Counters*, on page 17), but it doesn't really count the occurrences.

We all know that bioinformatics is the best thing since data science (which is the best thing since sliced bread). Bioinformatics deals with genome sequencing—figuring out the order of DNA nucleotides. Let's do some pseudo bioinformatics now and find out what kinds of nucleotides exist in a random DNA fragment:

```
dna = "AGTCCGCGAATACAGGCTCGGT"
dna_as_array = np.array(list(dna))
```

```
array(['A', 'G', 'T', 'C', 'C', 'G', 'C', 'G', 'A', 'A', 'T', 'A', 'C',
       'A', 'G', 'G', 'C', 'T', 'C', 'G', 'G', 'T'],
      dtype='<U1')
```

```
np.unique(dna_as_array)
```

```
array(['A', 'C', 'G', 'T'],
      dtype='<U1')
```

You knew it, didn't you?[2]

The function in1d(needle, haystack) returns a Boolean array where an element is True if the corresponding element of the needle is in the haystack. The arrays needle and haystack don't have to be of the same shape.

```
np.in1d(["MSFT", "MMM", "AAPL"], sap)
```

```
array([False, True, False], dtype=bool)
```

The functions union1d() and intersect1d() calculate the set theoretical union and intersection of two one-dimensional arrays. The arrays don't have to be of the same size, either. However, you may want to stick to the native Python set operators & and |. They are about twice as fast as their numpy brethren!

---

2. www.genomenewsnetwork.org/resources/whats_a_genome/Chp2_1.shtml

Unit 29

Saving and Reading Arrays

You will probably be using numpy not on its own, but as a powerful back end to pandas (Chapter 6, *Working with Data Series and Frames*, on page 83), networkx (Chapter 7, *Working with Network Data*, on page 121), and machine learning tools (Chapter 10, *Machine Learning*, on page 157). You will create numpy arrays from the data provided by low-level, data-processing tools, and deliver them to the higher-level analysis tools. It is unlikely you'll need to save or read numpy arrays directly.

However, just in case, numpy has a built-in facility for saving arrays to .npy files (function save(file, arr)) and reading previously saved arrays from .npy files (function load(file)). The files are in a binary format, and only numpy can handle them.

Both functions, perhaps recognizing their uselessness, are very friendly: file can be either an open file handle or a string file name, and if file is a file name without the .npy extension, the extension is added automatically.

```
# A silly way to copy an array
np.save("sap.npy", sap)
sap_copy = np.load("sap")
```

Another pair of functions, loadtxt() and savetxt(), loads tabular data from a text file and saves an array to a text file. numpy automatically creates the file, if needed, and opens it. numpy even goes as far as automatically zipping or unzipping the file content if the file name ends with .gz. You can control the way numpy handles commented lines and delimiters, and skips over unwanted rows:

```
arr = np.loadtxt(fname, comments="#", delimiter=None, skiprows=0,
                 dtype=float)
np.savetxt(fname, arr, comments="#", delimiter=" ", dtype=float)
```

Unit 30

Generating a Synthetic Sine Wave

It's time to impress our non-numpy friends and do something that data scientists normally don't do: generate a *synthetic sine wave*, a periodic signal that we could have captured using a cheap, imperfect, and noisy instrument with a limited range. The actual provenance of the signal and the nature of the instrument are not really important. Perhaps it was a voltmeter that you hooked into an electrical outlet, an outdoor digital thermometer that you left on your lawn on Sunday night and collected only on Friday, or even a stock market price ticker. (By the way, you can use synthetic periodic signals not just to impress friends, but also to test new digital signal processing algorithms.)

The generating code is as follows. numpy shines at its best in the highlighted portion of the code. That's where the vectorized magic happens: you create an array of sequential integer numbers, convert them to floating-point numbers, adjust to the right period, take the sine, magnify, displace, add Gaussian noise (see *Normal Distribution*, on page 149), and truncate the result as if measured by a limited-range instrument.

```
numpy_sinewave.py
# Import all good things
import numpy as np
import matplotlib.pyplot as plt
import matplotlib

# The constants define the signal, noise, and "instrument"
# properties
SIG_AMPLITUDE = 10; SIG_OFFSET = 2; SIG_PERIOD = 100
NOISE_AMPLITUDE = 3
N_SAMPLES = 5 * SIG_PERIOD
INSTRUMENT_RANGE = 9

➤ # Construct a sine wave and mix it with some random noise
➤ times = np.arange(N_SAMPLES).astype(float)
➤ signal = SIG_AMPLITUDE * np.sin(2 * np.pi * times / SIG_PERIOD) + SIG_OFFSET
➤ noise = NOISE_AMPLITUDE * np.random.normal(size=N_SAMPLES)
➤ signal += noise
➤
➤ # Truncate spikes that are outside of the instrument range
➤ signal[signal > INSTRUMENT_RANGE] = INSTRUMENT_RANGE
➤ signal[signal < -INSTRUMENT_RANGE] = -INSTRUMENT_RANGE

# Plot the results
```

```
matplotlib.style.use("ggplot")
plt.plot(times, signal)
plt.title("Synthetic sine wave signal")
plt.xlabel("Time")
plt.ylabel("Signal + noise")
plt.ylim(ymin = -SIG_AMPLITUDE, ymax = SIG_AMPLITUDE)

# Save the plot
plt.savefig("../images/signal.pdf")
```

The remaining, unhighlighted part of the code makes clever use of Matplotlib to visualize the noisy signal.

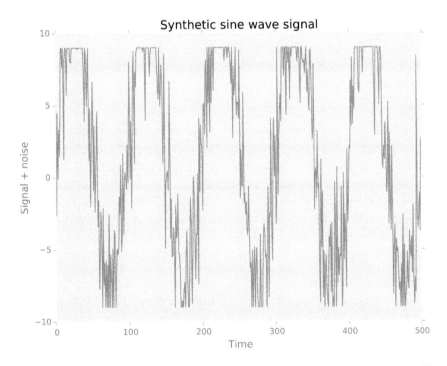

Matplotlib, numpy's sister package, will be at the focus of our attention in Chapter 8, *Plotting*, on page 135.

Your Turn

I hope I convinced you that numpy is an excellent toolset when it comes to number crunching. It treats vectors and matrices as first-class citizens; provides vectorized arithmetic, logical, and other operations; and provides a means for data reshaping, ordering, and aggregation. It even supplies a weird creature called nan, which is a number that is not a number. Can you tame some of the computationally intensive projects with numpy?

*Array Differentiator**

Partial sums are a rough equivalent of an integral. In fact, calculus defines an integral as an infinite sum of infinitesimal elements. Partial differences arr_{i+1}-arr_i are a rough equivalent of a derivative. numpy doesn't provide a tool for calculating partial array differences. Write a program that, given an array arr, calculates the partial differences of the array items. Assume that the array is numerical.

*HEI Locator***

Download the U.S. Higher Education Dataset from www.data.gov/education as a CSV file. Write a program that reports ten higher education institutions (HEIs) that are the closest geographically to the point defined by the mean latitude and mean longitude of all HEIs in the data set. Calculate the distances in degrees. Try to use numpy for data storage and processing as much as possible. Remember that the first row of the CSV file contains column headers, and that some fields or entire records in the file may be invalid.

*State Similarity Calculator***

The U.S. Census Bureau provides a summary of state-to-state population flows (download the most recent XLS file from www.census.gov/hhes/migration/data/acs/state-to-state.html and convert it to CSV by opening in Excel or OpenOffice Calc and exporting as CSV). Write a program that reports ten most similar pairs of states with respect to people migration. Consider two states X and Y similar if more than P_X/N people moved from X to Y, where $P_{X/Y}$ is the total flow out of X, and N is the total number of states and territories, less the territory of origin itself. Try to use numpy for data storage and processing as much as possible. Are both states in each pair typically on the same coast?

The art galleries of Paris contain the finest
collection of frames I ever saw.

> *Humphry Davy, Cornish chemist and inventor*

## CHAPTER 6

Working with Data Series and Frames

Data scientists traditionally admire tabular data (arrays, vectors, matrices). Tabular data is nicely shaped and can be conveniently accessed both element-wise and by rows and columns. Supercomputers and many modern high-end personal computers provide vectorized arithmetic operations that are performed on many or all tabular items at once (you saw a numpy implementation of them in Unit 24, *Broadcasting*, on page 71). However, numpy fails to tie numerical data itself with the data attributes: column and row names and indexes. This lack of references makes working with a set of more than one numpy array a real challenge.

Enter pandas.

The purpose of the pandas module is to add to Python the abstractions of data series and frames that are the core of the rival R language—the original language of data science. pandas is built on top of numpy and greatly extends and partially re-implements its functionality.

A pandas data frame is essentially a "smart" spreadsheet: a labeled table with columns (variables), observations (rows), and a multitude of built-in operations. (A series is simply a frame with only one column.) The data part of the table (the cells) is implemented as a numpy array. Many operations (such as data reshaping and aggregation and universal functions) also resemble their numpy counterparts. Row and column labels provide convenient, no-nonsense access to individual rows and columns. Furthermore, labeled rows and columns allow pandas programmers (us) to combine frames by merging and concatenating in "vertical" (stacking) and "horizontal" (side-by-side) directions. In this sense, frames act like relational database tables. (To refresh your knowledge of relational databases, revisit Chapter 4, *Working with Databases*, on page 47.)

Last but not least, pandas is nicely integrated with pyplot—a Python-based plotting and data visualization system, which we'll look at in Unit 41, *Basic Plotting with PyPlot*, on page 136. Honestly, pandas is all you need to do data science—in addition to all other tools, of course.

In this chapter, we'll start our pandas journey by looking at two pandas containers: Series and DataFrame in Unit 31, *Getting Used to Pandas Data Structures*, on page 85.

Unit 31

Getting Used to Pandas Data Structures

The module pandas adds two new containers to the already rich Python set of data structure: Series and DataFrame. A *series* is a one-dimensional, labeled (in other words, indexed) vector. A *frame* is a table with labeled rows and columns, not unlike an Excel spreadsheet or MySQL table. Each frame column is a series. With a few exceptions, pandas treats frames and series similarly.

Frames and series are not simply storage containers. They have built-in support for a variety of data-wrangling operations, such as:

- Single-level and hierarchical indexing

- Handling missing data

- Arithmetic and Boolean operations on entire columns and tables

- Database-type operations (such as merging and aggregation)

- Plotting individual columns and whole tables

- Reading data from files and writing data to files

Frames and series should be used whenever you deal with one- or two-dimensional tabular data. They are simply too convenient not to be used.

Series

A series is a one-dimensional data vector. Just like numpy arrays (you can find more on them on page 64), series are homogeneous: all series items must belong to the same data type.

You can create a simple series from any sequence: a list, a tuple, or an array. Let's use a tuple of recent U.S. inflation data to illustrate a pandas data series. But first, a disclaimer: I packed the previously calculated inflation data into a tuple to stress its immutable nature; aside from that, the following example requires no advanced knowledge of economics or finance!

```
import pandas as pd
# The last value is wrong, we will fix it later!
inflation = pd.Series((2.2, 3.4, 2.8, 1.6, 2.3, 2.7, 3.4, 3.2, 2.8, 3.8, \
                       -0.4, 1.6, 3.2, 2.1, 1.5, 1.5))
```

```
⇒  0      2.2
⇒  1      3.4
⇒  2      2.8
⇒  3      1.6
⇒  4      2.3
⇒  5      2.7
⇒  6      3.4
⇒  7      3.2
⇒  8      2.8
⇒  9      3.8
⇒  10    -0.4
⇒  11     1.6
⇒  12     3.2
⇒  13     2.1
⇒  14     1.5
⇒  15     1.5
⇒  dtype: float64
```

The built-in function len() is Python's universal yardstick. It works for series, too:

```
len(inflation)
```

```
⇒  16
```

One Series, Two Series, Three Series...

 The word *series* comes in both the singular and the plural form. It traces back to the Latin *serere*, which means *join* or *connect*.

A simple series, like the one you just created, has a default integer index: the first item's label is 0, the second is 1, and so on. The values attribute of a series has the list of all series values; the index attribute refers to the index of the series (Index is yet another pandas data type); and the index.values attribute refers to the array of all index values.

```
inflation.values
```

```
⇒  array([ 2.2,  3.4,  2.8,  1.6,  2.3,  2.7,  3.4,  3.2,  2.8,
⇒          3.8, -0.4,  1.6,  3.2,  2.1,  1.5,  1.5])
```

```
inflation.index
```

```
⇒  Int64Index([0, 1, 2, 3, 4, 5, 6, 7, 8, 9, 10, 11, 12, 13, 14, 15],
⇒     dtype='int64')
```

```
inflation.index.values
```

⇒ **array([0, 1, 2, 3, 4, 5, 6, 7, 8, 9, 10, 11, 12, 13, 14, 15])**

Note how pandas avoids reinventing the wheel and makes use of numpy arrays as its underlying storage!

Somewhat surprising, all these arrays (and the series attributes that they represent) are mutable. Changing values, index, and index.values actually changes the series values and the index. Let's use this fact to fix the last inflation item, which is wrong:

```
inflation.values[-1] = 1.6
```

The problem with the series is that it looks like an array and acts like an array and, according to the "duck test," is a duck—that is, an array. For example, it's hard to tell which year the first series item refers to. You could create another series of years and keep the two series together, but someone taught me in high school that parallel series are a sure path to an eventual disaster. So, let's create a series with a customized index by passing a dictionary to the Series constructor. The dictionary keys become the series index—an indivisible part of the series:

```
inflation = pd.Series({1999 : 2.2, «more items», 2014 : 1.6, 2015 : np.nan})
```

⇒ **1999   2.2**
⇒ **«more items»**
⇒ **2014   1.6**
⇒ **2015   NaN**

Alternatively, you can create a new index from any sequence and then attach it to an existing series:

```
inflation.index = pd.Index(range(1999, 2015))
inflation[2015] = numpy.nan
```

⇒ **1999   2.2**
⇒ **«more items»**
⇒ **2014   1.6**
⇒ **2015   NaN**

Series values and the index can have names, which are accessed and assigned through the namesake attributes. The names are essentially a form of documentation to remind us (and future core readers) about the nature of both sequences:

```
inflation.index.name = "Year"
inflation.name = "%"
```

```
⇒  Year
⇒  1999    2.2
⇒  «more items»
⇒  2014    1.6
⇒  2015    NaN
⇒  Name: %, dtype: float64
```

You can look at the entire series, with the index and all the names, either by printing it or typing its name on the command line in interactive mode, or by calling the functions head() and tail(), which return the first five and the last five rows of a series, respectively:

```
inflation.head()
```

```
⇒  Year
⇒  1999    2.2
⇒  2000    3.4
⇒  2001    2.8
⇒  2002    1.6
⇒  2003    2.3
⇒  Name: %, dtype: float64
```

```
inflation.tail()
```

```
⇒  Year
⇒  2011    3.2
⇒  2012    2.1
⇒  2013    1.5
⇒  2014    1.6
⇒  2015    NaN
⇒  Name: %, dtype: float64
```

Should you prefer a picture (worth a thousand words) to the head() and tail(), see the figure on page 89. (We'll learn about appropriate plotting tools in Chapter 8, *Plotting*, on page 135.)

Series are great for recording observations of one variable. However, many data sets have more than one variable. That's where frames come in.

Frames

A data frame is a table with labeled rows and columns. You can construct a frame from a two-dimensional numpy array, a list of tuples, a Python dictionary, or another frame. In the dictionary case, the keys serve as column names, and the values (which must be sequences) are column values. In the case of another frame, pandas copies column names from the source frame to the new frame. In the case of an array, you can supply the column names through the optional parameter columns (a sequence of column names). Following the

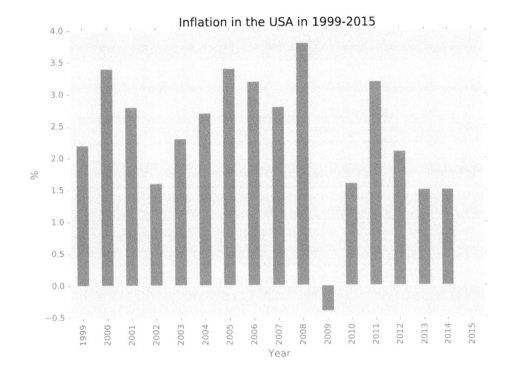

numpy approach, the frame index is called axis 0 ("vertical" dimension), and frame columns are called axis 1 ("horizontal" dimension).

Let's use a 2011 surveillance report by the National Institute on Alcohol Abuse and Alcoholism[1] to study frames. The report shows per capita alcohol consumption per state, per category (beer, wine, and spirits), and per year between 1977–2009.

NIAAA Report

 The NIAAA report is such an excellent source of data that I included a preprocessed copy of it as a "code" item for you to explore. But remember: do not drink and do data science!

You can create a simple frame with column names and an index by passing a list of row tuples or other sequences of the same length to the constructor. (Here I used a pandas CSV reader from Unit 37, *Taming Pandas File I/O*, on page 116 to create the full frame alco and then selected a one-year timespan.)

---

1.   pubs.niaaa.nih.gov/publications/surveillance92/CONS09.pdf

```
alco2009 = pd.DataFrame([(1.20, 0.22, 0.58),
                         (1.31, 0.54, 1.16),
                         (1.19, 0.38, 0.74),
                         «more rows»],
                        columns=("Beer", "Wine", "Spirits"),
                        index=("Alabama", "Alaska", «more states»))
```

```
⇒           Beer  Wine  Spirits
⇒ Alabama  1.20  0.22     0.58
⇒ Alaska   1.31  0.54     1.16
⇒ Arizona  1.19  0.38     0.74
⇒ «more rows»
```

You can also use a dictionary of columns to the same effect:

```
alco2009 = pd.DataFrame({"Beer" :   (1.20, 1.31, 1.19, «more rows»),
                         "Wine" :   (0.22, 0.54, 0.38, «more rows»),
                         "Spirits" : (0.58, 1.16, 0.74, «more rows»)},
                        index=("Alabama", "Alaska", «more states»))
```

Individual frame columns can be accessed using either dictionary or object notation. However, to add a new column, you must use the dictionary notation. If the object notation is used, pandas will create a new frame attribute instead. Just like with series, frames have a head() and a tail(). (Real pandas have tails, too!)

```
alco2009["Wine"].head()
```

```
⇒ State
⇒ Alabama       0.22
⇒ Alaska        0.54
⇒ Arizona       0.38
⇒ Arkansas      0.17
⇒ California     0.55
⇒ Name: Wine, dtype: float64
```

```
alco2009.Beer.tail()
```

```
⇒ State
⇒ Virginia        1.11
⇒ Washington      1.09
⇒ West Virginia   1.24
⇒ Wisconsin       1.49
⇒ Wyoming         1.45
⇒ Name: Beer, dtype: float64
```

And just like series, frames support broadcasting: you can assign a value to all rows of a column in one assignment statement. The column doesn't even have to exist; if it doesn't, pandas will create it.

```
alco2009["Total"] = 0
alco2009.head()
```

	Beer	Wine	Spirits	Total
State				
Alabama	1.20	0.22	0.58	0
Alaska	1.31	0.54	1.16	0
Arizona	1.19	0.38	0.74	0
Arkansas	1.07	0.17	0.60	0
California	1.05	0.55	0.73	0

The totals shown here are clearly wrong, but we'll find out how to fix them soon in *Arithmetic Operations*, on page 109.

Unit 32

Reshaping Data

The main contribution of pandas to the tabular data cause is data labeling: association of numerical or textual labels with columns (column names) and rows (flat and hierarchical indexes). This association is flexible: if you change the shape of the underlying numpy array (see the function reshape() on page 67) to make it match other frames, some rows may become columns, and columns may become rows. For example, if a hierarchical index of one frame has two levels (say, "Year" and "State"), but another frame has a flat "State" index, you will convert the "Year" labels into column names. In this unit, you will learn about flat and hierarchical indexing and reindexing, and other ways to reorganize data labels.

Indexing

A frame index is a collection of labels assigned to the frame rows. (The labels have to belong to the same data type, but don't have to be unique.) You can supply an index through the optional parameter index to the DataFrame() constructor. And just like in the case of a series, you can access and change column names and the index through the attributes index.values and columns.values.

```
alco2009.columns.values
```

⇒ `array(['Beer', 'Wine', 'Spirits', 'Total'], dtype=object)`

```
alco2009.index.values
```

⇒ `array(['Alabama', 'Alaska', 'Arizona', «...»], dtype=object)`

Any column in a frame can become an index—the functions reset_index() and set_index(column) are responsible for deposing the existing index, if any, and declaring a new one, respectively. Both functions return a new frame, but if you supply the optional parameter inplace=True, the functions modify the object frame itself:

```
alco2009.reset_index().set_index("Beer").head()
```

```
⇒              State  Wine  Spirits  Total
⇒ Beer
⇒ 1.20        Alabama  0.22    0.58      0
⇒ 1.31         Alaska  0.54    1.16      0
⇒ 1.19        Arizona  0.38    0.74      0
⇒ 1.07       Arkansas  0.17    0.60      0
⇒ 1.05     California  0.55    0.73      0
```

A frame index is an important row access tool and a relevant row identifier. Whatever column you use as the index, it must make sense. In the latter example, the column used does not: beer consumption is a property of a state, but not an identifier.

Once the index is in place, you can access individual rows through the row index attribute ix, which is like a dictionary of row series, keyed by the index labels. The frame columns serve as each series' index:

```
alco2009.ix["Nebraska"]
```

```
⇒ Beer       1.46
⇒ Wine       0.20
⇒ Spirits    0.68
⇒ Total      0.00
⇒ Name: Nebraska, dtype: float64
```

The Python operator in checks if a row with a certain label is present in the frame at all:

```
"Samoa" in alco2009.index
```

```
⇒ False
```

The function drop() returns a copy of a frame with a row or list of rows removed. To remove the rows in the original frame, pass the optional parameter inplace=True.

Reindexing

Reindexing creates a new frame or series from an existing frame or series by selecting possibly permuted rows, columns, or both. Essentially, it's a counterpart of numpy "smart" indexing (which we looked at in Unit 23, *Indexing and Slicing*, on page 69), except that if pandas doesn't find the requested row or column labels in the original frame, it will create a new row or column and populate it (or them) with nans.

In the next example, we create a list of states whose names begin with "S" (including "Samoa," which is not a state and is not in the alco2009 frame). Then we take all frame columns, except for the last one ("Total," which is not properly initialized, anyway), and add another column named "Water." Finally, we extract the selected rows and columns from the original frame. Because one row and one column don't exist, pandas creates them:

```
s_states = [state for state in alco2009.index if state[0] == 'S'] + ["Samoa"]
drinks = list(alco2009.columns) + ["Water"]
nan_alco = alco2009.reindex(s_states, columns=drinks)
```

```
⇒                 Beer  Wine  Spirits  Water
⇒ State
⇒ South Carolina  1.36  0.24     0.77    NaN
⇒ South Dakota    1.53  0.22     0.88    NaN
⇒ Samoa            NaN   NaN      NaN    NaN
```

The optional parameter method with possible values "ffill" and "bfill" forward fills or backward fills—*imputes*—the missing values. (This works only on monotonically decreasing or increasing indexes.) You'll learn more about data imputation on page 98.

Hierarchical Indexing

pandas supports hierarchical (multilevel) indexes and hierarchical (multilevel) column names. The multilevel indexes are also known as multiindexes.

A multilevel index consists of three lists:

- Level names
- All possible labels per level
- Lists of actual values for each item in the frame or series (the lengths of the lists are the same and equal to the number of levels in the index)

The following frame contains a complete version of the NIAAA data set, not just for the year 2009. It has a multiindex both by state and year and is sorted by both indexes: first by "State," then by "Year."

```
alco
```

```
⇒               Beer  Wine  Spirits
⇒ State    Year
⇒ Alabama  1977  0.99  0.13     0.84
⇒          1978  0.98  0.12     0.88
⇒          1979  0.98  0.12     0.84
⇒          1980  0.96  0.16     0.74
⇒          1981  1.00  0.19     0.73
⇒ «...»
```

```
⇒  Wyoming 2005  1.21  0.23     0.97
⇒          2006  1.47  0.23     1.05
⇒          2007  1.49  0.23     1.10
⇒          2008  1.54  0.23     1.12
⇒          2009  1.45  0.22     1.10
```

Data transformation operations often produce hierarchical indexes, but you can construct them on purpose, too. The function MultiIndex.from_tuples() takes a collection of tuples with labels and an optional list of level names and produces a multiindex. You can attach the multiindex to an existing frame or series or pass it as a parameter to the DataFrame() constructor:

```
multi = pd.MultiIndex.from_tuples((
        ("Alabama", 1977), ("Alabama", 1978), ("Alabama", 1979), ...,
        ("Wyoming", 2009)),
        names=["State", "Year"])
```

```
⇒  MultiIndex(levels=[['Alabama', 'Alaska', «...», 'Wyoming'],
⇒                     [1977, 1978, 1979, 1980, «...», 2009]],
⇒             labels=[[0, 0, 0, 0, 0, 0, 0, 0, «...», 50],
⇒                     [0, 1, 2, 3, 4, 5, 6, 7, «...», 32]],
⇒             names=['State', 'Year'])
```

```
alco.index = multi
```

A multiindex can be used the same way as a flat index. A partial selection (by one of several labels) produces a frame; a complete selection produces a series.

```
alco.ix['Wyoming'].head()
```

```
⇒        Beer  Wine  Spirits
⇒  Year
⇒  1977  1.79  0.21     1.32
⇒  1978  1.82  0.22     1.36
⇒  1979  1.86  0.22     1.30
⇒  1980  1.85  0.24     1.32
⇒  1981  1.91  0.24     1.27
```

```
alco.ix['Wyoming', 1999]
```

```
⇒  Beer        1.41
⇒  Wine        0.18
⇒  Spirits     0.84
⇒  Name: (Wyoming, 1999), dtype: float64
```

pandas treats multilevel indexes and columns consistently—to the extent that an index level may become a column level and the other way around.

Stacking and Pivoting

You can fully or partially flatten a multilevel index—at the expense of introducing multilevel column names. You can fully or partially flatten multilevel column names—at the expense of introducing a multiindex.

The stack() function increments the number of levels in the index and simultaneously decrements the number of levels in the column names. It makes the frame taller and narrower, as shown in the following figure. If the column names are already flat, a series is returned. The unstack() function does just the opposite: it decrements the number of levels in the index and simultaneously increments the number of levels in the column names. It makes the frame shorter and wider. If the index is already flat, a series is returned.

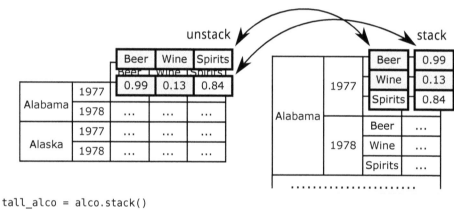

```
tall_alco = alco.stack()
tall_alco.index.names += ["Drink"]
tall_alco.head(10)
```

```
State    Year  Drink
Alabama  1977  Beer      0.99
               Wine      0.13
               Spirits   0.84
         1978  Beer      0.98
               Wine      0.12
               Spirits   0.88
         1979  Beer      0.98
               Wine      0.12
               Spirits   0.84
         1980  Beer      0.96
dtype: float64
```

The result of the previous operation is a series with a three-level index (I had to provide the name for the missing third level—"Drink").

```
wide_alco = alco.unstack()
wide_alco.head()
```

	Beer										...
Year	1977	1978	1979	1980	1981	1982	1983	1984	1985	1986	...
State											...
Alabama	0.99	0.98	0.98	0.96	1.00	1.00	1.01	1.02	1.06	1.09	...
Alaska	1.19	1.39	1.50	1.55	1.71	1.75	1.76	1.73	1.68	1.68	...
Arizona	1.70	1.77	1.86	1.69	1.78	1.74	1.62	1.57	1.67	1.77	...
Arkansas	0.92	0.97	0.93	1.00	1.06	1.03	1.03	1.02	1.03	1.06	...
California	1.31	1.36	1.42	1.42	1.43	1.37	1.37	1.38	1.32	1.36	...

```
[5 rows x 99 columns]
```

The result of the previous operation is a frame with a flat index and two-level, hierarchical column names. You'll often find these kinds of frames in CSV and other tabular files. You may want to stack them to make the data "more square" and easier to manage.

Stacking and unstacking are special cases of a more general operation—*pivoting*. The pivot(index,columns,values) function converts a frame into another frame using column index as the new index, columns as the new list of column names, and column values as the data.

In the following example, alco is reorganized into a "square" frame describing wine consumption by year (new flat index) and state (column names):

```
alco.pivot("Year", "State", "Wine")
```

State	Alabama	Alaska	Arizona	Arkansas	California	Colorado	Connecticut
Year							
1977	0.13	0.42	0.34	0.10	0.67	0.36	0.35
1978	0.12	0.45	0.37	0.11	0.68	0.47	0.38
1979	0.12	0.47	0.39	0.10	0.70	0.47	0.40
1980	0.16	0.50	0.36	0.12	0.71	0.47	0.43
«...»							

```
[33 rows x 51 columns]
```

If index is None, pandas reuses the original frame index.

Unit 33

Handling Missing Data

Data is almost never perfect. Some values are firm (no need to worry about them); some are questionable (you've got to treat them with a grain of salt); and some are simply missing.

pandas traditionally uses numpy.nan (explained on page 74) to represent missing data—probably so as to not confuse it with any number and because its name resembles the NA ("Not Available") symbol from the R language. pandas also provides functions for recognizing and imputing missing values.

There are several reasons values may be missing in series and frames: you may have never collected them; you may have collected them but discarded them as inappropriate; or you may have combined several complete data sets, but their combination was not a complete data set anymore. Unfortunately, you can't do any serious data analysis before you take care of the missing values. You must either delete or impute them—replace with some values that make sense. Let's find out how.

Deleting Missing Data

The simplest way to handle missing data is to pretend you never had it in the first place (the "See No Evil, Hear No Evil" approach). The dropna() function removes partially (how="any", default) or fully (how="all") invalid columns (axis=0, default) or rows (axis=1) and returns a "clean" copy of the object frame. You can use the optional parameter inplace=True to modify the original frame instead of creating a copy.

```
nan_alco.dropna(how="all")
```

```
⇒                  Beer  Wine  Spirits  Water
⇒ State
⇒ South Carolina  1.36  0.24     0.77    NaN
⇒ South Dakota    1.53  0.22     0.88    NaN
```

```
nan_alco.dropna(how="all", axis=1)
```

```
⇒                  Beer  Wine  Spirits
⇒ State
⇒ South Carolina  1.36  0.24     0.77
⇒ South Dakota    1.53  0.22     0.88
⇒ Samoa            NaN   NaN      NaN
```

You cannot remove a missing value alone without destroying the frame grid. You can remove only the whole row or column containing the "dirty" cell, and the resulting "clean" frame may be totally empty. Instead of seeing no evil, you will see no data.

```
nan_alco.dropna()
```

⇒ **Empty DataFrame**
⇒ **Columns: [Beer, Wine, Spirits, Water]**
⇒ **Index: []**

Imputing Missing Data

Another way to deal with missing values is to impute the missing data. Imputing missing values means replacing them with some "clean" values that make sense. What makes sense, of course, depends on what kind of data it is. Only we, data scientists, can tell whether the replacement is appropriate or not.

Two most common imputation techniques are replacing with a constant (a zero, a one, and so on) and replacing with an average taken across the "clean" values. But first, you need to identify what's actually missing.

The functions isnull() and notnull() are complementary. They return True if a value is a nan or not a nan, respectively. Note that according to the IEEE 754 floating-point standard, the expression np.nan==np.nan is False, which makes a direct comparison impossible!

```
nan_alco.isnull()
```

	Beer	Wine	Spirits	Water
State				
South Carolina	False	False	False	True
South Dakota	False	False	False	True
Samoa	True	True	True	True

```
nan_alco.notnull()
```

	Beer	Wine	Spirits	Water
State				
South Carolina	True	True	True	False
South Dakota	True	True	True	False
Samoa	False	False	False	False

Let's fix the "Spirits" column by imputing the average (remember that - [hyphen] is numpy's idea of a negation operator):

```
sp = nan_alco['Spirits'] # Selected a column with dirty rows
clean = sp.notnull() # The clean rows
sp[-clean] = sp[clean].mean() # Impute the clean mean into the dirty rows
nan_alco
```

	Beer	Wine	Spirits	Water
State				
South Carolina	1.36	0.24	0.770	NaN
South Dakota	1.53	0.22	0.880	NaN
Samoa	NaN	NaN	0.825	NaN

You have to impute the means on a column-by-column (or row-by-row) basis, but you can impute constants across the frame. The function fillna(val) in its simplest form imputes val into the "holes." Alternatively, the function propagates the last valid observation along its column (axis=0}, default) or row (axis=1) either forward (method="ffill") or backward (method="bfill"). The function returns a new frame or series, unless you specify the parameter inplace=True.

```
nan_alco.fillna(0)
```

	Beer	Wine	Spirits	Water
State				
South Carolina	1.36	0.24	0.77	0
South Dakota	1.53	0.22	0.88	0
Samoa	0.00	0.00	0.00	0

```
nan_alco.fillna(method="ffill")
```

	Beer	Wine	Spirits	Water
State				
South Carolina	1.36	0.24	0.77	NaN
South Dakota	1.53	0.22	0.88	NaN
Samoa	1.53	0.22	0.88	NaN

Replacing Values

Another way to handle specific "dirty" values is to replace them selectively by "clean" values on a case-by-case basis. The replace(val_or_list,new_val) function replaces one value or a list of values by another value or a list of values. If you use lists, they must be of the same length. The function returns a new frame or series, unless you pass the inplace=True parameter.

The function combine_first(pegs) combines two frames or two series. It replaces the missing values in the object frame/series by the corresponding values from the argument frame/series. In a sense, the argument serves as a source of default values.

Unit 34

Combining Data

Once your data is in a series or frames, you may need to combine the data to prepare for further processing, as some data may be in one frame and some in another. pandas provides functions for merging and concatenating frames —as long as you know whether you want to merge or to concatenate.

Merging

Merging frames is similar to merging database tables: pandas combines rows with identical indexes (or identical values in other designated columns) from the left and right frames. When there is only one match in the right frame for each row in the left frame, that type of merging is called *one-to-one*. When there is more than one match, that type of merging is called *one-to-many*. In that case, pandas replicates the rows of the left frame as needed, and the replication may cause row duplication (but we look at how to deal with this on page 104). When there are several matches for some rows in each of the frames, that type of merging is called *many-to-many*, and again, pandas replicates rows as needed and inserts numpy.nans into the "holes."

If both frames have a column with the same name (the key column), you can merge the frames on that column. If not, you can designate other columns as the keys, as shown here:

```
df = pd.merge(df1, df2, on="key")
df = pd.merge(df1, df2, left_on="key1", right_on="key2")
```

Use U.S. Census Bureau data[2] to build a frame with the U.S. population as of July 1, 2009. In addition to the state-by-state data, the frame has observations for East, Northeast, Northwest, Midwest, West, South, and the U.S. as a whole.

```
population.head()
```

	Population
State	
Wyoming	544270
District of Columbia	599657
Vermont	621760
North Dakota	646844
Alaska	698473

---

2.   www.census.gov/popest/data/historical/2000s/vintage_2009/state.html

Because both population and alco2009 are indexed by "State," you can remove the indexes, merge both frames on all common columns, and observe the population side-by-side with alcohol consumption:

```
df = pd.merge(alco2009.reset_index(),
            population.reset_index()).set_index("State")
df.head()
```

```
⇒            Beer  Wine  Spirits  Population
⇒ State
⇒ Alabama    1.20  0.22    0.58    4708708
⇒ Alaska     1.31  0.54    1.16     698473
⇒ Arizona    1.19  0.38    0.74    6595778
⇒ Arkansas   1.07  0.17    0.60    2889450
⇒ California  1.05  0.55    0.73   36961664
```

If two frames have columns with identical names, pandas adds the suffixes "_l" and "_r" to the columns' names. The optional parameter suffixes (a tuple of two strings) controls the suffixes. If you want to merge on indexes rather than general columns, use the optional parameters left_index=True and/or right_index=True. The result of the following statement is the same as the one previous, but the default sorting order may be different:

```
df = pd.merge(alco2009, population, left_index=True, right_index=True)
df.head()
```

```
⇒                       Beer  Wine  Spirits  Population
⇒ State
⇒ Wyoming               1.45  0.22    1.10     544270
⇒ District of Columbia  1.26  1.00    1.64     599657
⇒ Vermont               1.36  0.63    0.70     621760
⇒ North Dakota          1.63  0.25    1.16     646844
⇒ Alaska                1.31  0.54    1.16     698473
```

If both indexes are designated as keys, you may want to use join() instead of merge():

```
population.join(alco2009).tail(10)
```

```
⇒                Population  Beer  Wine  Spirits
⇒ State
⇒ Illinois         12910409  1.22  0.39    0.73
⇒ Florida          18537969  1.21  0.48    0.92
⇒ New York         19541453  0.91  0.46    0.69
⇒ Texas            24782302  1.42  0.28    0.58
⇒ California        36961664  1.05  0.55    0.73
⇒ Northeast        55283679   NaN   NaN     NaN
⇒ Midwest          66836911   NaN   NaN     NaN
⇒ West             71568081   NaN   NaN     NaN
⇒ South           113317879   NaN   NaN     NaN
⇒ United States   307006550   NaN   NaN     NaN
```

Both functions join() and merge() take an optional parameter how with the acceptable values of "left" (default for join()), "right", "inner" (default for merge()), or "outer". Left join uses the calling (left) frame's index. Right join uses the parameter (right) frame's index. Outer join uses the union of the indexes. Inner join uses the intersection of the indexes. (pandas join types are consistent with MySQL join types that were introduced earlier in *Join*, on page 54.)

If the indexes of the frames are not identical, then left, right, and outer joins and merges introduce rows with missing values. In the previous example, this occurred where beer, wine, and spirits totals are not known. Inner join/merge never introduces new missing values.

If two frames have columns with identical names, then you must provide the optional parameters lsuffix (a string) and rsuffix (a string). pandas will append the suffixes to the names of the common columns.

The function join() can also take the optional parameter on and join two frames on a shared column name (but not on columns with different names or on a column and an index).

Concatenating

The concat() function concatenates a list of frames by placing them next to each other in one of the dimensions—"vertical" (axis=0, default) or "horizontal" (axis=1)—and returns a new frame:

```
pd.concat([alco2009, population], axis=1).tail()
```

```
                Beer  Wine  Spirits  Population
Washington      1.09  0.51     0.74     6664195
West             NaN   NaN      NaN    71568081
West Virginia   1.24  0.10     0.45     1819777
Wisconsin       1.49  0.31     1.16     5654774
Wyoming         1.45  0.22     1.10      544270
```

If the dimensions don't match, pandas adds additional rows or columns with missing values in the "holes."

pandas faithfully preserves the indexes of all vertically stacked frames, which may result in an index with duplicate keys. You can either live with this or delete duplicates (we'll learn how on page 104) or use the optional parameter keys (a list of strings) that adds the second-level index to the new frame, thus forming a hierarchical index. If you concatenate the frames "horizontally" (column-wise), the same parameter creates hierarchical column names.

Let's use data from the Statistics Canada website[3] to create a frame that has the population of Canadian provinces in 2011. Now we can create a new frame that describes both North American countries in a properly indexed way. (Remember that the U.S. frame is two years older than the Canadian one.)

```
pop_na = pd.concat([population, pop_ca], keys=["US", "CA"])
pop_na.index.names = ("Country", "State")
```

```
                                Population
Country State
US      Wyoming                     544270
        District of Columbia        599657
        Vermont                     621760
        North Dakota                646844
        Alaska                      698473
«...»
CA      Alberta                    3790200
        British Columbia           4499100
        Yukon                        35400
        Northwest Territories        43500
        Nunavut                      34200
```

Remember that the hierarchical index can be flattened if necessary.

To Merge or to Concatenate?

Both merge() and concat() combine two or more frames. Use concat() to combine frames that have similar content (such as populations of U.S. states and Canadian provinces: "apples to apples"). Use merge() to combine frames that have complementary content (such as populations and alcohol consumption rates: "apples to oranges").

Deleting Duplicates

The duplicated([subset]) function returns a Boolean series denoting if each row in all or subset (a list of column names) columns is duplicated. The optional parameter keep controls whether the "first", "last", or each (True) duplicate is marked.

The drop_duplicates() function returns a copy of a frame or series with duplicates from all or subset (a list of column names) columns removed. The optional parameter keep controls whether the "first", "last", or each (True) duplicate is removed. You can use the optional parameter inplace=True to remove duplicates from the original object.

---

3. www.statcan.gc.ca/tables-tableaux/sum-som/l01/cst01/demo02a-eng.htm

Unit 35

Ordering and Describing Data

Having the data in a frame is not enough. What we need next is a yardstick that ranks and describes the data that we have. The universal Python yard-stick, len(), and its brethren, min() and max(), are a good starting point, but often we want answers to more questions, aside from *How many?* and *How much?* pandas provides a number of functions for sorting, ranking, counting, membership testing, and getting descriptive statistics.

Sorting and Ranking

Series and frames can be sorted by index or by value (values). The sort_index() function returns a frame sorted by the index (it doesn't work for series). The sorting order is always lexicographic (numeric for numbers, alphabetic for strings), and you can use the ascending parameter (default True) to control it. The option inplace=True, as always, insists that pandas sorts the original frame.

```
population.sort_index().head()
```

```
⇒              Population
⇒ State
⇒ Alabama       4708708
⇒ Alaska         698473
⇒ Arizona       6595778
⇒ Arkansas      2889450
⇒ California    36961664
```

The sort_values() function returns a frame or a series sorted by values. In the case of a frame, the first parameter is a column name or a list of column names, and the optional parameter ascending can be a Boolean value or a list of Boolean values (one per column used for sorting). The parameter na_position ("first" or "last") specifies where to place the nans (at the beginning or at the end).

```
population.sort_values("Population").head()
```

```
⇒                        Population
⇒ State
⇒ Wyoming                  544270
⇒ District of Columbia     599657
⇒ Vermont                  621760
⇒ North Dakota             646844
⇒ Alaska                   698473
```

Did you know that Wyoming has the smallest population of any state in the United States? Now you do.

The rank() function computes a frame or a series of numerical ranks for each frame or series value. If several values are equal, the function assigns them all the average rank. The Boolean parameter numeric_only restricts ranking only to numeric values. The parameter na_option ("top", "bottom", or "keep") specifies how to treat nans: move them to the top or to the bottom of the result frame or keep them wherever they were in the original frame.

```
pop_by_state = population.sort_index()
pop_by_state.rank().head()
```

```
⇒              Population
⇒ State
⇒ Alabama            29
⇒ Alaska              5
⇒ Arizona            38
⇒ Arkansas           20
⇒ California         51
```

It's now just a matter of a dozen keystrokes to merge or join the latter output with the original population frame and have the actual population and state's rank in one frame.

Descriptive Statistics

Descriptive statistical functions calculate sum(), mean(), median(), standard deviation std(), count(), min(), and max() of a series or each column in a frame. Each of them can take the Boolean parameter skipna, which specifies if nans must be excluded from the analysis, and axis, which tells the function which way to go ("vertically" or "horizontally").

```
alco2009.max()
```

```
⇒ Beer       1.72
⇒ Wine       1.00
⇒ Spirits    1.82
⇒ dtype: float64
```

```
alco2009.min(axis=1)
```

```
⇒ State
⇒ Alabama       0.22
⇒ Alaska        0.54
⇒ Arizona       0.38
⇒ Arkansas      0.17
⇒ California     0.55
⇒ dtype: float64
```

```
alco2009.sum()
```

⇒ **Beer   63.22**
⇒ **Wine   19.59**
⇒ **Spirits   41.81**
⇒ **dtype: float64**

The functions argmax() (for series) and idxmax() (for frames) find the index positions of the first occurrences of the maximal values. It's easy to remember these two functions: these are the only two functions in pandas that don't treat series and frames consistently.

pandas has limited support for pseudo-integration, pseudo-differentiation, and other cumulative methods. The functions cumsum(), cumprod(), cummin(), and cummax() calculate cumulative sums, products, minimums, and maximums, starting from the first item in the series or each frame column. You can get the cumulative alcohol consumption in Hawaii (or in any other state, for that matter) with cumsum():

```
alco.ix['Hawaii'].cumsum().head()
```

⇒	Beer	Wine	Spirits	Total
⇒ Year				
⇒ 1977	1.61	0.36	1.26	3.23
⇒ 1978	2.99	0.82	2.56	6.37
⇒ 1979	4.59	1.26	3.84	9.69
⇒ 1980	6.24	1.72	5.05	13.01
⇒ 1981	7.98	2.16	6.21	16.35

The diff() function calculates the running difference between the consecutive column/series items. The first row of the result is undefined. With diff(), you can find the yearly change of alcohol consumption in Hawaii, too:

```
alco.ix['Hawaii'].diff().head()
```

⇒	Beer	Wine	Spirits	Total
⇒ Year				
⇒ 1977	NaN	NaN	NaN	NaN
⇒ 1978	-0.23	0.10	0.04	-9.000000e-02
⇒ 1979	0.22	-0.02	-0.02	1.800000e-01
⇒ 1980	0.05	0.02	-0.07	-4.440892e-16
⇒ 1981	0.09	-0.02	-0.05	2.000000e-02

The name of the last column is misleading after the pseudo-differentiation. You may want to change it to "Δ(Total)," "Change of Total," or something else to avoid confusion in the future.

Uniqueness, Counting, Membership

numpy can treat arrays as sets (as discussed on page 78). pandas can treat series as sets, too (but not frames). Let's blow the dust off the pseudo bioinformatics example we started on page 78 and practice our serious series set skills:

```
dna = "AGTCCGCGAATACAGGCTCGGT"
dna_as_series = pd.Series(list(dna), name="genes")
dna_as_series.head()
```

```
⇒  0    A
⇒  1    G
⇒  2    T
⇒  3    C
⇒  4    C
⇒  Name: genes, dtype: object
```

The functions unique() and value_counts() compute an array of distinct values from the series and a frame with the counts of each distinct value (compare with Counter on page 17), respectively. If the series contains nans, they are included in the count.

```
dna_as_series.unique()
```

```
⇒  array(['A', 'G', 'T', 'C'], dtype=object)
```

```
dna_as_series.value_counts().sort_index()
```

```
⇒  A    5
⇒  C    6
⇒  G    7
⇒  T    4
⇒  Name: genes, dtype: int64
```

The isin() function is defined for both pandas principal data types. It returns a Boolean series or frame of the same size specifying whether each series/frame item is a member of a certain collection. We know that only nucleotides A, C, G, and T are allowed in a DNA sequence. Are *all* our nucleotides valid?

```
valid_nucs = list("ACGT")
dna_as_series.isin(valid_nucs).all()
```

```
⇒  True
```

At this point, you're probably so comfortable with the data that you can't wait until you can do some number crunching and perhaps even get some cool results. The tools to transform data are just around the corner on page 109.

Unit 36

Transforming Data

Now you're ready to have a look at the pandas "powerhouse": vectorized arithmetic, logical operations, and other data transformation mechanisms.

Arithmetic Operations

pandas supports the four arithmetic operations (addition, subtraction, multiplication, and division) and numpy universal functions (or *ufuncs*, which were explained on page 73). The operators and functions can be used to combine frames of the same size and structure, frame columns and series, and series of the same size.

We're finally in the position to correct the "Total" column of the alco frame:

```
alco["Total"] = alco.Wine + alco.Spirits + alco.Beer
alco.head()
```

		Beer	Wine	Spirits	Total
State	Year				
Alabama	1977	0.99	0.13	0.84	1.96
	1978	0.98	0.12	0.88	1.98
	1979	0.98	0.12	0.84	1.94
	1980	0.96	0.16	0.74	1.86
	1981	1.00	0.19	0.73	1.92

If you want to measure total consumptions on a logarithmic scale, numpy conveniently serves log10(), log(), and many other ufuncs:

```
np.log10(alco.Total).head()
```

State	Year	
Alabama	1977	0.292256
	1978	0.296665
	1979	0.287802
	1980	0.269513
	1981	0.283301
Name: Total, dtype: float64		

All arithmetic operations preserve indexing. This feature is called *data alignment*: if you add two series, pandas adds an item with the index "C" in one series to the namesake item in the other series. If the namesake item is missing, the result is a nan. Let's genetically engineer two more DNA fragments by cunningly removing the C and T nucleotides from the original fragment on page 108, and then count the nucleotides by type in both fragments:

```
dna = "AGTCCGCGAATACAGGCTCGGT"
dna1 = dna.replace("C", "")
dna2 = dna.replace("T", "")
dna_as_series1 = pd.Series(list(dna1), name="genes") # No C's
dna_as_series2 = pd.Series(list(dna2), name="genes") # No T's
dna_as_series1.value_counts() + dna_as_series2.value_counts()
```

```
⇒ A    10
⇒ C    NaN
⇒ G    14
⇒ T    NaN
⇒ Name: genes, dtype: float64
```

Check the data. Perhaps it's time to do some missing data cleanup (Unit 33, *Handling Missing Data*, on page 98) before proceeding to data aggregation?

Data Aggregation

Data aggregation is a three-step procedure during which data is split, aggregated, and combined:

1. At the split step, the data is split by key or keys into chunks.

2. At the apply step, an aggregation function (such as sum() or count()) is applied to each chunk.

3. At the combine step, the calculated results are combined into a new series or frame.

The power of pandas is in the groupby() function and a collection of aggregation functions, which actually execute the three steps listed here automatically so that all we have to do is sit tight and enjoy our coffee.

The groupby() function splits a frame by collecting the rows in groups based on the values of one or more categorical keys. The function returns a group generator that you can use in a loop (to access the content of the groups) or in conjunction with an aggregation function.

The list of aggregation functions includes count() (returns the number of rows in the group); sum() (returns the sum of numerical rows in the group); mean(), median(), std(), and var() (each returns the namesake statistical measure of rows in the group); min() and max() (returns the smallest and the largest row in the group); prod() (returns the product of numerical rows in the group); and first() and last() (returns the first and the last row in the group; this function is meaningful only if the frame is ordered).

Let's tap into our good old alco frame and get the total alcohol consumption in all states by year:

```
# We want to group by the "Year" column
alco_noidx = alco.reset_index()
sum_alco = alco_noidx.groupby("Year").sum()
sum_alco.tail()
```

```
⇒         Beer   Wine  Spirits   Total
⇒  Year
⇒  2005  63.49  18.06    38.89  120.44
⇒  2006  64.37  18.66    40.15  123.18
⇒  2007  64.67  19.08    40.97  124.72
⇒  2008  64.67  19.41    41.59  125.67
⇒  2009  63.22  19.59    41.81  124.62
```

If you use more than one column for splitting, the result has a multiindex with the levels corresponding to each column.

You can also access the content of each group by iteration over the groups in a for loop. At each iteration, the generator returned by the groupby() function supplies the index entry and the group of rows that corresponds to the entry (as a frame):

```
for year, year_frame in alco_noidx.groupby("Year"):
  «do_something(year, year_frame)»
```

Sometimes you may wish you could group rows by a computable property rather than by the existing column or columns. pandas allows data aggregation through mappings using dictionaries or series. Let's consider a dictionary that maps states to the regions defined by the U.S. Census Bureau:[4]

```
state2reg
```

```
⇒ {'Idaho': 'West', 'West Virginia': 'South', 'Vermont': 'Northeast', «...»}
```

Now you can calculate mean alcohol consumption by region! Remember that the dictionary operates on the row index labels, not values, so assign the appropriate column as the frame index (at least temporarily, for the duration of the grouping operation). The dictionary values (which are incidentally also group names) become the index of the returned frame:

```
alco2009.groupby(state2reg).mean()
```

```
⇒                 Beer      Wine   Spirits
⇒  Midwest    1.324167  0.265000  0.822500
⇒  Northeast  1.167778  0.542222  0.904444
⇒  South      1.207500  0.275625  0.699375
⇒  West       1.249231  0.470769  0.843846
```

---

4. www2.census.gov/geo/docs/maps-data/maps/reg_div.txt

Using the terminology incorrectly attributed to William of Ockham, an English Franciscan friar and scholastic philosopher and theologian,[5] *data aggregation abridges entities* and, therefore, is good for us. Discretization, on the contrary, *multiplies entities*: it converts a value into categories. It would be bad for us —unless it were very useful.

Discretization

Discretization refers to the conversion of a continuous variable to a discrete (*categorical*) variable often for the purpose of histogramming and machine learning (see Chapter 10, *Machine Learning*, on page 157).

The cut() function splits an array or series passed as the first parameter into half-open bins—categories. The second parameter is either a number of equally sized bins or a list of bins' edges. If the goal is to split the sequence into N bins, you would pass a list of N+1 bin edges. The categories produced by cut() belong to an ordinal data type: you can rank them and compare them to one another.

```
cats = pd.cut(alco2009['Wine'], 3).head()
```

```
⇒ State
⇒ Alabama         (0.0991, 0.4]
⇒ Alaska             (0.4, 0.7]
⇒ Arizona         (0.0991, 0.4]
⇒ Arkansas        (0.0991, 0.4]
⇒ California         (0.4, 0.7]
⇒ Name: Wine, dtype: category
⇒ Categories (3, object): [(0.0991, 0.4] < (0.4, 0.7] < (0.7, 1]]
```

If you prefer to mint your own category labels, pass another optional parameter labels (a list of N labels, one label per bin).

```
cats = pd.cut(alco2009['Wine'], 3, labels=("Low", "Moderate", "Heavy"'))
cats.head()
```

```
⇒ State
⇒ Alabama            Low
⇒ Alaska        Moderate
⇒ Arizona           Low
⇒ Arkansas          Low
⇒ California     Moderate
⇒ Name: Wine, dtype: category
⇒ Categories (3, object): [Low < Moderate < Heavy]
```

---

5. en.wikipedia.org/wiki/William_of_Ockham

If you set labels=False, cut() numbers the bins instead of labeling them and returns only the bin membership information:

```
cats = pd.cut(alco2009['Wine'], 3, labels=False).head()
```

```
⇒  State
⇒  Alabama        0
⇒  Alaska         1
⇒  Arizona        0
⇒  Arkansas       0
⇒  California      1
⇒  Name: Wine, dtype: int64
```

The qcuts() function is similar to cuts(), but operates in terms of quantiles, not bin widths. You can use it to calculate quantiles (such as the median and quartiles).

```
quants = pd.qcut(alco2009['Wine'], 3, labels=("Low", "Moderate", "Heavy"))
quants.head()
```

```
⇒  State
⇒  Alabama             Low
⇒  Alaska            Heavy
⇒  Arizona        Moderate
⇒  Arkansas            Low
⇒  California         Heavy
⇒  Name: Wine, dtype: category
⇒  Categories (3, object): [Low < Moderate < Heavy]
```

Another way to discretize a variable with a small number of possible values (that variable is already categorical!) is to decompose it into a set of dummy *indicator* variables—one variable per possible value.

A dummy variable is a Boolean variable that is true for one value of a categorical variable and false for all other values. Dummy variables are used in logit regression (discussed on page 163) and in other forms of machine learning, which are discussed in Chapter 10, *Machine Learning*, on page 157.

The get_dummies() function converts an array, series, or frame to another frame with the same index as the original object and each column representing a dummy variable. If the object is a frame, use the optional parameter columns (the list of columns to be discretized).

Remember the state breakdown by regions that we prepared on page 111? Here's another way to look at it through the lens of indicators:

```
pd.get_dummies(state2reg).sort_index().head()
```

state	Midwest	Northeast	South	West
Alabama	0	0	1	0
Alaska	0	0	0	1
Arizona	0	0	0	1
Arkansas	0	0	1	0
California	0	0	0	1

Because each state belongs exactly to one region, the sum of all values in each row is always one. This is true for any set of dummies, not just for the states.

Mapping

Mapping is the most general form of data transformation. It uses the map() function to apply an arbitrary one-argument function to each element of a selected column. The function can be either a built-in Python function, a function from any imported module, a user-defined function, or an anonymous lambda function.

As an example, let's create three-letter abbreviations of state names.

```
with_state = alco2009.reset_index()
abbrevs = with_state["State"].map(lambda x: x[:3].upper())
abbrevs.head()
```

```
0    ALA
1    ALA
2    ARI
3    ARK
4    CAL
Name: State, dtype: object
```

Naturally, our attempt to create unique three-letter abbreviations failed, but it was worth it!

Unlike the highly optimized and parallelized universal functions, the function passed as the parameter to map() is executed by the Python interpreter and cannot be optimized. This makes map() quite inefficient. Use it only when no other options are feasible.

Cross-Tabulation

Cross-tabulation computes group frequencies and returns a frame with rows and columns representing different values of two categorical variables (factors). If you supply the optional parameter margins=True, the function also calculates rows and columns subtotals.

The following code fragment calculates the joint frequencies of a state being or not being a "wine state" (consuming more wine than average) vs. being or not being a "beer state" (consuming more beer than average):

```
wine_state = alco2009["Wine"] > alco2009["Wine"].mean()
beer_state = alco2009["Beer"] > alco2009["Beer"].mean()
pd.crosstab(wine_state, beer_state)
```

```
⇒ Beer     False  True
⇒ Wine
⇒ False      14     15
⇒ True       12     10
```

If the numbers in the table are not that different (they are not!), the two factors are likely to be independent. We'll come back to this observation in *Calculating Statistical Measures*, on page 153.

Unit 37

Taming Pandas File I/O

If you had no other reason to use pandas, you might still succumb to its mastery of file input and output. pandas input/output facilities enable data exchange between frames and series on one hand, and CSV files, tabular files, fixed-width files, JSON files (earlier discussed on page 36), the operating system clipboard, and so on, on the other hand. Among other things, pandas supports:

- Automatic indexing and column names extraction
- Data type inference, data conversion, and missing data detection
- Datetime parsing
- The elimination of "unclean" data (skipping rows, footers, and comments; treating thousands' separators)
- Data chunking

Reading CSV and Tabular Files

The read_csv() function reads a frame from a CSV file designated by name or from an open file handle. With almost fifty optional parameters, this function is a CSV Swiss Army knife; we certainly will use it instead of the CSV reader() (which we looked at on page 34; perhaps it's time to unlearn them?). Some important optional parameters are:

- sep or delimiter—the column delimiter. read_csv() accepts regular expressions here (for example, r"\s+" for "any number of white spaces").
- header—the row number to use as column names. Pass None if you have your own list of column names.
- index_col—the column name to use as the index. If you pass False, pandas will generate a default numeric index.
- skiprows—the number of rows at the beginning of the file or a list of row numbers to skip.
- thousands—the character used as the thousands separator in large numbers.
- names—a list of column names.

- na_values—a string or a list of strings to treat as missing data. If you want to use different strings for different columns (for example, "n/a" for string data and -1 for numeric data), you can put them in a dictionary as values, keyed by the column names.

Let's go over the process of importing a list of U.S. states and Census Bureau regions (first mentioned on page 111). The original CSV file has a regular but sparse structure:

```
Northeast,New England,Connecticut
,,Maine
,,Massachusetts
,,New Hampshire
,,Rhode Island
,,Vermont
Northeast,Mid-Atlantic,New Jersey
,,New York
,,Pennsylvania
«more states»
```

It doesn't have a header row and has many empty cells, but we know how to fill in both the column names and the empties:

```
regions = pd.read_csv("code/regions.csv",
                      header=None,
                      names=("region", "division", "state"))
state2reg_series = regions.ffill().set_index("state")["region"]
state2reg_series.head()
```

⇒ **state**
⇒ **Connecticut   Northeast**
⇒ **Maine   Northeast**
⇒ **Massachusetts   Northeast**
⇒ **New Hampshire   Northeast**
⇒ **Rhode Island   Northeast**
⇒ **Name: region, dtype: object**

The original state2reg is a dictionary, not a series, but pandas seems to have conversion functions literally for every occasion:

```
state2reg = state2reg_series.to_dict()
```

⇒ **{'Washington': 'West', 'South Dakota': 'Midwest', «more states»}**

The function to_csv() writes a frame or a series back to a CSV file.

The function read_table() reads a frame from a tabular file designated by name or from an open file handle. Essentially, it's a read_csv() in disguise with the default separator being a tab space, not a comma.

Chunking

If you ever want to read tabular data from a large file in pieces (chunks), you need chunking. If you need chunking, simply pass the parameter chunksize (number of lines) to the function read_csv(). Instead of actually reading the lines, the function returns a generator that you can use in a for loop.

Let the file code/regions_clean.csv have the same data as code/regions.csv but without region and division omissions. Let's pretend that the file is *really* big, and we are scared of reading it all at once. The following code fragment creates a TextFileReader object for iteration and an accumulator series and reads the CSV file five lines at a time. For each piece, the column "region" is extracted, and the values in the column are counted. Then the counts are added to the accumulator. If a certain key doesn't exist in the accumulator yet, simply set it to 0 via the optional parameter fill_value to avoid nans.

```
chunker = pd.read_csv("code/regions_clean.csv", chunksize=5,
                      header=None, names=("region", "division", "state"))
accum = pd.Series()
for piece in chunker:
  counts = piece["region"].value_counts()
  accum = accum.add(counts, fill_value=0)
accum
```

```
⇒ Midwest      12
⇒ Northeast     9
⇒ South        17
⇒ West         13
⇒ dtype: float64
```

Reading Other Files

The read_json() function attempts to read a frame from a JSON file. Because JSON files are not in general tabular but have a hierarchical structure, coercing JSON data to a rectangular format is not always possible.

The read_fwf() function reads a frame from a file with fixed-width data. The function uses either colspecs (a list of tuples with the start and end+1 positions of a column in a line) or widths (a list of column widths).

The read_clipboard() function reads text from the system clipboard and then passes it to read_table(). You can use this function for one-time extraction of tables from web pages by copying them to the clipboard.

Your Turn

pandas frames and series are convenient data containers that add an extra level of abstraction and consistency on top of numpy arrays. Frames and series are great for importing and exporting data from and to tabular files; structuring, restructuring, merging, and aggregating data; and performing simple and advanced arithmetic operations on it. And, unlike the R language frames, the size of pandas frames is limited only by your imagination, not by the size of your computer's RAM.

Lynx Trappings[*]

Write a program that uses the annual Canadian lynx trappings data[6] and reports total lynx trappings by decade (ten years), sorted in the reverse order (most "productive" decade first). The program should download the data file into the cache directory—but only if the file is not in the cache yet. If the directory doesn't exist, it will be created. The program should save the results as a CSV file in the directory doc. If the directory doesn't exist, it will be created.

GDP vs. Alcohol Consumption[**]

Wikipedia has plenty of data on various aspects of demographics, including alcohol consumption per capita[7] and GDP of countries and dependencies per capita.[8] Write a program that uses this data to cross-tabulate GDP level (above average vs. below average) vs. alcohol consumption level (above average vs. below average). Based on the table, do the two measures seem to be correlated?

Weather vs. Alcohol Consumption[***]

Combine the historic alcohol consumption data with the historical weather data by state. Use cross-tabulation to estimate if the drinking habits are possibly correlated with the average local temperatures and total precipitations. In other words, do people drink more when it rains and pours?

The website of the National Climatic Data Center[9] is a good starting point of your historical weather data quest.

---

6. vincentarelbundock.github.io/Rdatasets/csv/datasets/lynx.csv
7. en.wikipedia.org/wiki/List_of_countries_by_alcohol_consumption_per_capita
8. en.wikipedia.org/wiki/List_of_countries_by_GDP_(PPP)_per_capita
9. www.ncdc.noaa.gov/cdo-web/

Looking down, he surveyed the rest of his clothes,
which in parts resembled the child's definition of a net
as a lot of holes tied together with string...

> — *Morley Roberts, English novelist and short story writer*

CHAPTER 7

Working with Network Data

Network analysis is a recently new area of data analysis. Network science borrowed network theoretical methods partly from mathematics (graph theory), partly from social sciences, and a lot from sociology. Some people still refer to network analysis as "social network analysis," and who are we to judge them?

From a data science point of view, a network is a collection of interconnected objects. We can actually treat all kinds of numeric and non-numeric (text) objects as networks, as long as there is a way to interconnect them. Depending on our background and the field of study, we may call the network objects "nodes," "vertexes," or "actors," and call the connections between them "arcs," "edges," "links," or "ties." We may represent networks graphically and mathematically as graphs.

In this chapter, you'll learn how to create networks from network and non-network data, understand network measures, and analyze networks—in particular, how to calculate and interpret network node centralities and community structure. Our friendly assistants in this chapter are going to be the standard Anaconda module networkx and the community module that you should have installed before attempting community detection.[1]

---

1. pypi.python.org/pypi/python-louvain/0.3

Dissecting Graphs

Mathematically speaking, a graph is a set of nodes connected with edges. There are different kinds of edges, nodes, and graphs, and they are connected and interpreted in different ways. So, before we start dissecting graphs, let's start with some important definitions.

Graph Elements, Types, and Density

If at least one graph edge is *directed* (say, it connects node A to node B but not the other way around), the graph itself is directed and is called a *digraph*. If there are parallel edges in a graph (that is, node A may be connected to node B by more than one edge), the graph is called a *multigraph*. The edge from node A to itself is called a *loop*. A graph without loops and parallel edges is called a *simple* graph.

Weights can be assigned to graph edges. A weight is usually (but not necessarily) a number between 0 and 1, inclusive. The larger the weight, the stronger the connection between the nodes. A graph with weighted edges is called a *weighted* graph.

Edge weight is an example of an edge attribute. Edges may have other attributes, including numeric, Boolean, and string. Graph nodes can have attributes, too.

The degree of a graph node is defined as the number of edges connected (incident) to the node. For a directed graph, *indegree* (the number of edges coming into the node) and *outdegree* (the number of edges going out of the node) are distinguished.

Graph density d (0≤d≤1) tells how close the graph is to a *complete* graph—a cobweb of all possible edges. For example, for a directed graph with e edges and n nodes:

$$d = \frac{e}{n(n-1)}$$

For an undirected graph:

$$d = \frac{2e}{n(n-1)}$$

Graph Structure

Graphs and the networks that they induce are exciting, diverse, and multi-faceted objects. To understand them better, it's important to understand the terminology.

The concept of inter-node connectivity can be expanded by looking at graph walks. A *walk* is any sequence of edges such that the end of one edge is the beginning of another edge. When we take a bus from node "home" to node "subway station A," then take a train from node "subway station A" to node "subway station B," and then walk from node "subway station B" to node "our office," we complete a graph walk (even though only part of the walk involves actual walking). We call a walk that doesn't intersect itself (in other words, it doesn't include the same node twice, except perhaps for the first-last node) a *path*. We call a closed path a *loop*. It's a loop that takes us back home at the end of a hard day.

Just like we can measure the distance between two objects in real life, we can measure the distance between any two graph nodes: it is simply the smallest number of edges (sometimes called "hops") in any path connecting the nodes. This definition doesn't work in the case of weighted graphs, but sometimes you can pretend that the graph is really not weighted, and still count the edges. In a directed graph, the distance from A to B is not always equal to the distance from B to A. In fact, we may be able to get from A to B, but not back! Living your life from birth to death is a sad but sobering example.

The largest distance between any two nodes in a graph is called the *diameter* (D) of the graph. Unlike circles, graphs don't have area.

A connected component, or simply a component, is a set of all nodes in a graph such that there is a path from each node in the set to each other node in the set. For a directed graph, strongly connected components (connected by actual paths) and weakly connected components (connected by the paths where the edges were converted to undirected) are distinguished.

If a graph has several components, the largest component is called the *giant connected component* (GCC). Quite often the size of the GCC is huge. When this is the case, it's often best to work with the GCC rather than with the entire graph to avoid non-connectivity issues.

Sometimes two parts of a graph are connected, but the connection is so subtle that the removal of a single edge breaks the graph apart. Such an edge is called a *bridge*.

A *clique* is a set of nodes such that each node is directly connected to each other node in the set. D'Artagnan and Three Musketeers formed a clique, and so does any other band that operates under the "all for one and one for all" principle. We call the largest clique in a graph the *maximum clique*. If a clique cannot be enlarged by adding another node to it, it is called a *maximal clique*. A maximum clique is always a maximal clique, but the converse is not always true. A complete graph is a maximal clique.

A *star* is a set of nodes such that one node is connected to all other nodes in the set, but the other nodes are not connected to each other. Stars are commonly found in hierarchical multilevel systems (for example, corporations, military institutions, and the Internet).

A set of nodes directly connected to a node A is called the *neighborhood* (G(A) of A). Neighborhoods are a key part in *snowballing*, which is a data acquisition technique whereby the edges of a randomly selected seed node are followed to its neighbors, then to the neighbors of the neighbors (a second-degree neighborhood), and so on.

The local clustering coefficient of a node A (also known as simply the clustering coefficient) is the number CC(A) of edges in A's neighborhood (excluding the edges directly connected to A), divided by the maximum possible number of edges. In other words, it's the density of the neighborhood of A without the node A itself. The clustering coefficient of any node in a star is 0. The clustering coefficient of any node in a complete graph is 1. CC(A) can be used as a measure of star likeness or completeness of G(A).

A network *community* is a set of nodes such that the number of edges interconnecting these nodes is much larger than the number of edges crossing the community boundary. *Modularity* ($m \in [-1/2, 1]$) is a measure of quality of community structure. It's defined as the fraction of the edges that fall within the community minus the expected such fraction if edges were distributed at random. High modularity ($m \approx 1$) characterizes a network with dense and clearly visible communities. Identifying such communities is perhaps the most important outcome of network data analysis (and we take a look at that next in Unit 39, *Network Analysis Sequence*, on page 126).

Centralities

Centrality is a measure of the importance of a node in a network. There are several types of centrality measures that measure different aspects of importance. For convenience, centralities are often scaled to the range between 0 (an unimportant, peripheral node) and 1 (an important, central node).

Degree

> Degree centrality of A is the number of neighbors of A, which is the same as the degree of A or the size of G(A). You can scale it by dividing by the maximum possible number of neighbors of A, n-1.

Closeness

> Closeness centrality of A is the reciprocal of the average shortest path length L_{BA} from all other nodes to A:

$$cc_A = \frac{n-1}{\sum_{B \neq A} L_{BA}}$$

Betweenness

> Betweenness centrality of A is the fraction of all shortest paths between all pairs of nodes in the network, excluding A, that contain A.

Eigenvector

> Eigenvector centrality of A is defined recursively as the scaled sum of the eigenvector centralities of all neighbors of A:

$$ec_A = \frac{1}{\lambda} \sum_{B \in G(A)} ec_B$$

The last two centrality measures are computationally expensive, and it may not be practical to calculate them for large networks.

Unit 39

Network Analysis Sequence

Now that you're armed with proper definitions and formulas, let's have a look at the big picture of network data analysis.

A typical network analysis sequence consists of the following steps:

1. It starts with identifying discrete entities and the relations between them. The entities become the network nodes, and the relations become edges. If the relations are binary (present vs. absent), they directly define the network edges. If the relations are continuous or discrete, but not binary, you can either treat them as weighted edges or convert them into unweighted edges, but only if the value of the relation is at or above a threshold. The latter transformation is called *sampling*. The sampling threshold is chosen based on empirical and pragmatic considerations. If the threshold is too high, the network is too sparse and falls apart into many small components; if the threshold is too low, the network loses any community structure and becomes a tangle.

2. Various network measures are calculated: density, number of components, GCC size, diameter, centralities, clustering coefficients, and so on.

3. Network communities are identified. If the network ends up being modular, you can assign labels to the communities, replace the communities with "supernodes," and study the new induced network.

4. Finally, just like in any other data science experiment, results are interpreted, and a report with a lot of appealing pictures is produced.

The module networkx supplies almost everything you need for a typical network study, with one major exception: the pictures it produces are not only not appealing, but, frankly, quite pathetic. For a better visualization, turn to Gephi (see the sidebar on page 131).

Unit 40

Harnessing Networkx

The networkx module contains essential tools for creating, modifying, exploring, plotting, exporting, and importing networks. It supports simple and directed graphs and multigraphs. You will learn how to construct and modify a network by adding and removing nodes, edges, and attributes; how to calculate various network measures (such as centralities); and how to explore network community structure.

Building and Fixing a Network

Let's use Wikipedia data[2] to construct and explore a network of nation states, based on the presence (and length) of international land borders. The network graph is undirected; it contains no loops and no parallel edges.

```
import networkx as nx

borders = nx.Graph()
not_borders1 = nx.DiGraph() # Just for our reference
not_borders2 = nx.MultiGraph() # Just for our reference
```

You can modify an existing network graph by adding or removing individual nodes or edges, or groups of nodes or edges. When you remove a node, all incident edges are removed, too. When you add an edge, its end nodes are added, too, unless they already existed in the graph. You can label nodes with either numbers or strings:

```
borders.add_node("Zimbabwe")
borders.add_nodes_from(["Lugandon", "Zambia", "Portugal", "Kuwait",
                        "Colombia"])
borders.remove_node("Lugandon")
borders.add_edge("Zambia", "Zimbabwe")
borders.add_edges_from([("Uganda", "Rwanda"), ("Uganda", "Kenya"),
                        ("Uganda", "South Sudan"), ("Uganda", "Tanzania"),
                        ("Uganda", "Democratic Republic of the Congo")])
```

After all of the territories and the connections between them are added, you get an easy-to-read graph, as shown in the figure on page 128.

---

2. en.wikipedia.org/wiki/List_of_countries_and_territories_by_land_borders

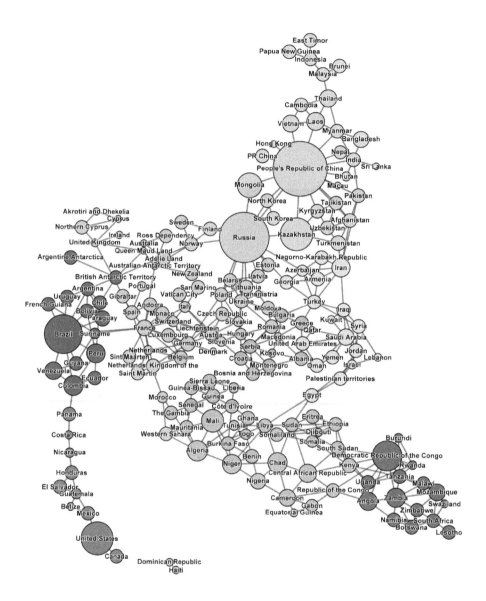

Node size in the graph represents total land border length, and the different colors correspond to network communities (which will be introduced on page 132).

Finally, the clear() function removes all nodes and edges from a graph. You are unlikely to use it very often.

Exploring and Analyzing a Network

Network analysis and exploration with networkx is as simple as calling a number of functions and looking into the values of few attributes. Given the abundance of references to the built-in len() function in this book, you should not be even remotely surprised that applying it to a graph returns the graph "length" (the number of nodes):

```
len(borders)
```

⇒ **181**

The actual node lists are available through the function nodes() and the attributes node and edge (the latter attribute also contains the edge dictionaries). Both attributes are read-only; you cannot add edges or nodes by making changes to them. (Even if you try to, networkx will not record the changes.) The edge list is also available through the function edges():

```
borders.nodes()
```

⇒ **['Iran', 'Palestinian territories', 'Chad', 'Bulgaria', 'France', «...»]**

```
borders.node
```

⇒ **{{'Iran': {'L': 5440.0}, 'Palestinian territories': {},**
⇒ ** 'Chad': {'L': 5968.0}, 'Bulgaria': {'L': 1808.0}, «...»}**

The dictionaries show the node attributes (which in our case is the total length of the land borders):

```
borders.edge
```

⇒ **{'Iran': {'Nagorno-Karabakh Republic': {}, 'Turkey': {}, 'Pakistan': {},**
⇒ ** 'Afghanistan': {}, 'Iraq': {}, 'Turkmenistan': {}, 'Armenia': {},**
⇒ ** 'Azerbaijan': {}}, «...»}**

The attribute edge is a dictionary of dictionaries with one entry per node. It also contains edge attributes (such as "weight"), if any.

```
borders.edges()[:5]
```

⇒ **[('Iran', 'Nagorno-Karabakh Republic'), ('Iran', 'Turkey'),**
⇒ ** ('Iran', 'Pakistan'), ('Iran', 'Afghanistan'), ('Iran', 'Iraq')]**

You can obtain the list of neighbors of a node through the neighbors() function:

```
borders.neighbors("Germany")
```

⇒ **['Czech Republic', 'France', 'Netherlands, Kingdom of the', 'Denmark',**
⇒ ** 'Switzerland', 'Belgium', 'Netherlands', 'Luxembourg', 'Poland', 'Austria']**

You can compute the degree, indegree, and outdegree of a node from the length of its respective neighborhood or by calling the functions degree(), indegree(), or outdegree(). When you call these functions with no parameters, they return a dictionary of the degrees indexed by the node labels. When you call them with a node label as the parameter, they return the degree of that node.

```
borders.degree("Poland")
```

⇒ 7

```
borders.degree()
```

⇒ {'Iran': 8, 'Nigeria': 4, 'Chad': 6, 'Bulgaria': 5, 'France': 14,
⇒ 'Lebanon': 2, 'Namibia': 4, «...»}

So, which country has the most neighbors?

```
degrees = pandas.DataFrame(list(borders.degree().items()),
                columns=("country", "degree")).set_index("country")
degrees.sort("degree").tail(4)
```

⇒ Country
⇒ Brazil   11
⇒ Russia   14
⇒ France   14
⇒ People's Republic of China   17

A Big Kit for a Big Network

It's not uncommon to work with Really Large Networks. (How about the Facebook social graph with 1.59 billion nodes, for starters?) Just like everything implemented in pure Python, networkx is not known for its high performance. Enter NetworKit, a highly efficient and parallelizable network analysis toolkit. NetworKit developers claim that "community detection in a 3 billion edge web graph can be performed on a 16-core server in a matter of minutes"[3]— something the community module can only dream about. What's best, NetworKit is integrated with matplotlib, scipy, numpy, pandas, and networkx, which makes it even more attractive.

The clustering coefficient is undefined for directed graphs, but you can explicitly turn a directed graph into an undirected graph, if needed. The function clustering() returns a dictionary of all clustering coefficients of the clustering coefficient of a particular node:

---

3.   networkit.iti.kit.edu

```
nx.clustering(not_borders1) # Doesn't work for a directed network!
nx.clustering(nx.Graph(not_borders1)) # Would work!
nx.clustering(borders)
```

⇒ **{'Iran': 0.2857142857142857, 'Nigeria': 0.5, 'Chad': 0.4, 'Bulgaria': 0.4,**
⇒ **'France': 0.12087912087912088, 'Lebanon': 1.0, 'Namibia': 0.5, «...»}**

```
nx.clustering(borders, "Lithuania")
```

⇒ **0.8333333333333334**

The connected_components(), weakly_connected_components(), and strongly_connected_com-
ponents() functions return a list generator of respective connected components
(as node label lists) from the graph. You can use the generator in an iterator
expression (for loop or list comprehension) or convert it to a list with the built-
in list() function. If you need a subgraph defined by the node list n from the
graph G, you can extract it with the function subgraph(G, n). Alternatively, you
can use a family of functions connected_component_subgraphs(), and so on, to calculate the connected components and get them as a graph list generator:

```
list(nx.weakly_connected_components(borders)) # Doesn't work!
list(nx.connected_components(borders)) # Works!
```

⇒ **[{'Iran', 'Chad', 'Bulgaria', 'Latvia', 'France', 'Western Sahara', «...»}]**

```
[len(x) for x in nx.connected_component_subgraphs(borders)]
```

⇒ **[179, 2]**

Gephi It!

Gephi is "an interactive visualization and exploration platform for
all kinds of networks and complex systems."[4] Some call it "the
Paintbrush of network analysis." Despite networkx having its own
graph visualization support (via matplotlib, which is discussed in
Unit 41, *Basic Plotting with PyPlot*, on page 136), I prefer to use Gephi
because of its versatility and instant feedback.

All centrality functions return either a dictionary of centralities, indexed by
the node labels, or individual node centralities. These dictionaries are excellent
building blocks for pandas data frames and indexed series. The following
comments show which country has the highest centrality in the respective
category:

---

4. gephi.org

```
nx.degree_centrality(borders) # People's Republic of China
nx.in_degree_centrality(borders)
nx.out_degree_centrality(borders)
nx.closeness_centrality(borders) # France
nx.betweenness_centrality(borders) # France
nx.eigenvector_centrality(borders) # Russia
```

Managing Attributes

A networkx graph, as well as its node and edge attributes, are implemented as dictionaries. A graph has a dictionary interface to the nodes. A node has a dictionary interface to its edges. An edge has a dictionary interface to its attributes. You can pass attribute names and values as optional parameters to the functions add_node(), add_nodes_from(), add_edge(), and add_edges_from():

```
# Edge attribute
borders["Germany"]["Poland"]["weight"] = 456.0
# Node attribute
borders.node["Germany"]["area"] = 357168
borders.add_node("Penguinia", area=14000000)
```

When the nodes() and edges() functions are called with the optional parameter data=True, they return a list of all nodes or edges with all of their attributes:

```
borders.nodes(data=True)
```

⇒ `[«...», ('Germany', {'area': 357168}), «...»]`

```
borders.edges(data=True)
```

⇒ `[('Uganda', 'Rwanda', {'weight': 169.0}),`
⇒ ` ('Uganda', 'Kenya', {'weight': 933.0}),`
⇒ ` ('Uganda', 'South Sudan', {'weight': 435.0}), «...»]`

Cliques and Community Structure

The find_cliques() and isolates() functions detect maximal cliques and isolates (zero-degree nodes). find_cliques() is not implemented for directed graphs (a digraph is coerced to an undirected graph first); it returns a node list generator, as shown here:

```
nx.find_cliques(not_borders1) # Not implemented for digraphs!
nx.find_cliques(nx.Graph(not_borders1)) # Would work!
list(nx.find_cliques(borders))
```

⇒ `[['Iran', 'Nagorno-Karabakh Republic', 'Armenia', 'Azerbaijan'],`
⇒ ` ['Iran', 'Afghanistan', 'Pakistan'], «...»]`

```
nx.isolates(borders)
```

⇒ `['Penguinia']`

The module for community detection, community, is not a part of Anaconda—it must be installed separately. The module does not support digraphs.

The best_partition() function uses the Louvain method and returns a community partition—a dictionary of numeric community labels indexed by the node labels. The modularity() function reports the modularity of the partition:

```
import community
partition = community.best_partition(borders)
```

⇒ `{'Uganda': 0, 'Zambia': 1, 'Portugal': 2, 'Bulgaria': 2, «...»}`

```
community.modularity(partition, borders)
```

⇒ `0.7462013020754683`

If the modularity is too low (≪0.5), the network does not have a clear community structure—at least one you shouldn't rely on.

Input and Output

A family of read and write functions read network data from files and write data to files. It is our responsibility to open and close the files (and create, if necessary). Some functions require that the files are opened in binary mode. Consult the following table to find out what some of these functions are.

Type	Read	Write	File extension
Adjacency list	read_adjlist(f)	write_adjlist(G, f)	Not specified
Edge list	read_edgelist(f)	write_edgelist(G, f)	Not specified
GML	read_gml(f)	write_gml(G, f)	.gml
GraphML	read_graphml(f)	write_graphml(G, f)	.graphml
Pajek	read_pajek(f)	write_pajek(G, f)	.net

Table 4—Some **networkx** Input and Output Functions

```
with open("borders.graphml", "wb") as netfile:
  nx.write_pajek(borders, netfile)
with open("file.net", "rb") as netfile:
  borders = nx.read_pajek(netfile)
```

Not all file formats support all network features. You can read more about different formats and features at the Gephi website[5] to help you choose the right output format for your graphs!

---

5.   gephi.org/users/supported-graph-formats/

Your Turn

Network analysis is extremely contagious. Once you learn it, you start seeing networks everywhere, even in Shakespeare.[6] Thinking in terms of networks, centralities, and communities adds another layer of sophistication to your data analysis skills, so don't hesitate to strengthen them by practicing.

Centrality Correlations[*]

Download a social network graph of select Epinions.com users from the Stanford Large Network Dataset Collection (prepared by J. Leskovec and A. Krevl),[7] and extract the tenth largest community. Write a program that calculates and displays pairwise correlations between all network centrality measures mentioned in this chapter (you can also add a clustering coefficient for more fun). I suggest that you store all centralities in a pandas data frame. You may need to read about how to calculate correlations in pandas in *Calculating Statistical Measures*, on page 153.

Are any pairs of centralities strongly correlated?

Shakespeare Works[**]

The complete works of William Shakespeare are available from MIT.[8] Write a program that creates a network of all the plays and the 100 top-most frequently used non–stop word stems. A stem and a play are connected if the stem is used in the play, and the weight of the edge equals the frequency of use. The program then identifies network communities and reports the modularity and the member nodes by community.

To the best of your knowledge of Shakespeare, does the reported partition make sense?

Border Network[**]

Use Wikipedia data, networkx, and Gephi to reconstruct the network of states and borders, including nodes sizes and communities (assign node attributes that could later be used in Gephi for node sizing and coloring).

---

6. www.slideshare.net/DmitryZinoviev/desdemona-52994413
7. snap.stanford.edu/data/soc-Epinions1.html
8. shakespeare.mit.edu

"I am plotting for myself, and counterplotting the designs of others,"
replied Tresham, mysteriously.

  ➤ William Harrison Ainsworth, English historical novelist

CHAPTER 8

Plotting

Plotting data is an essential part of any exploratory or predictive data analysis —and probably the most essential part of report writing. Frankly speaking, nobody wants to read reports without pictures, even if the pictures are irrelevant, like this elegant sine wave:

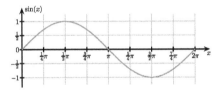

There are three principal approaches to programmable plotting. We start an *incremental* plot with a blank plot canvas and then add graphs, axes, labels, legends, and so on, incrementally using specialized functions. Finally, we show the plot image and optionally save it into a file. Examples of incremental plotting tools include the R language function plot(), the Python module pyplot, and the gnuplot command-line plotting program.

Monolithic plotting systems pass all necessary parameters, describing the graphs, charts, axes, labels, legends, and so on, to the plotting function. We plot, decorate, and save the final plot at once. An example of a monolithic plotting tool is the R language function xyplot().

Finally, *layered* tools represent what to plot, how to plot, and any additional features as virtual "layers"; we add more layers as needed to the "plot" object. An example of a layered plotting tool is the R language function ggplot(). (For the sake of aesthetic compatibility, the Python module matplotlib provides the ggplot plotting style.)

In this chapter, you'll take a look at how to do incremental plotting with pyplot.

Basic Plotting with PyPlot

Plotting for numpy and pandas is provided by the module matplotLib—namely, by the sub-module pyplot.

Let's start our experimentation with pyplot by invoking the spirit of the NIAAA surveillance report you converted into a frame earlier on page 88, and proceed to plotting alcohol consumption for different states and alcohol kinds over time. Unfortunately, as is always the case with incremental plotting systems, no single function does all of the plotting, so let's have a look at a complete example:

```
pyplot-images.py
import matplotlib, matplotlib.pyplot as plt
import pickle, pandas as pd

# The NIAAA frame has been pickled before
alco = pickle.load(open("alco.pickle", "rb"))
del alco["Total"]
columns, years = alco.unstack().columns.levels

# The state abbreviations come straight from the file
states = pd.read_csv(
    "states.csv",
    names=("State", "Standard", "Postal", "Capital"))
states.set_index("State", inplace=True)

# Alcohol consumption will be sorted by year 2009
frames = [pd.merge(alco[column].unstack(), states,
                   left_index=True, right_index=True).sort_values(2009)
          for column in columns]

# How many years are covered?
span = max(years) - min(years) + 1
```

The first code fragment simply imports all necessary modules and frames. It then combines NIAAA data and the state abbreviations into one frame and splits it into three separate frames by beverage type. The next code fragment is in charge of plotting.

```
pyplot-images.py
# Select a good-looking style
matplotlib.style.use("ggplot")

STEP = 5
# Plot each frame in a subplot
for pos, (draw, style, column, frame) in enumerate(zip(
        (plt.contourf, plt.contour, plt.imshow),
        (plt.cm.autumn, plt.cm.cool, plt.cm.spring),
        columns, frames)):

    # Select the subplot with 2 rows and 2 columns
    plt.subplot(2, 2, pos + 1)

    # Plot the frame
    draw(frame[frame.columns[:span]], cmap=style, aspect="auto")

    # Add embellishments
    plt.colorbar()
    plt.title(column)
    plt.xlabel("Year")
    plt.xticks(range(0, span, STEP), frame.columns[:span:STEP])
    plt.yticks(range(0, frame.shape[0], STEP), frame.Postal[::STEP])
    plt.xticks(rotation=-17)
```

The functions imshow(), contour(), and contourf() (at ❶) display the matrix as an image, a contour plot, and a filled contour plot, respectively. Don't use these three functions (or any other plotting functions) in the same subplot, because they superimpose new plots on the previously drawn plots—unless that's your intention, of course. The optional parameter cmap (at ❸) specifies a pre-built palette (color map) for the plot.

You can pack several subplots of the same or different types into one master plot (at ❷). The function subplot(n, m, number) partitions the master plot into n virtual rows and m virtual columns and selects the subplot number. The subplots are numbered from 1, column-wise and then row-wise. (The upper-left subplot is 1, the next subplot to the right of it is 2, and so on.) All plotting commands affect only the most recently selected subplot.

Note that the origin of the image plot is in the upper-left corner, and the Y axis goes down (that's how plotting is done in computer graphics), but the origin of all other plots is in the lower-left corner, and the Y axis goes up (that's how plotting is done in mathematics). Also, by default, an image plot and a contour plot of the same data have different aspect ratios, but you can make them look similar by passing the aspect="auto" option.

The functions colorbar(), title(), xlabel(), ylabel(), grid(), xticks(), yticks(), and tick_params() (at ❹) add the respective decorations to the plot. (We'll revisit them in Unit 43, *Mastering Embellishments*, on page 140.) The function grid() actually toggles the grid on and off, so whether you have a grid or not depends on whether you had it in the first place, which, in turn, is controlled by the plotting style.

The function tight_layout() adjusts subplots and makes them look nice and tight. Take a look at the following plots:

```
pyplot-images.py
plt.tight_layout()
plt.savefig("../images/pyplot-all.pdf")
#plt.show()
```

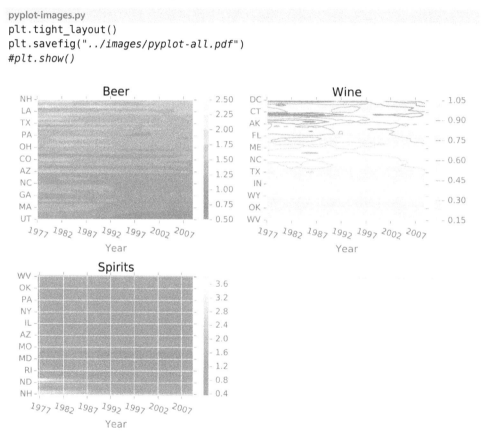

The function savefig() saves the current plot in a file. The function takes either a file name or an open file handle as the first parameter. If you pass the file name, savefig() tries to guess the image format from the file extension. The function supports many popular image file formats, but not GIF.

The function show() displays the plot on the screen. It also clears the canvas, but if you simply want to clear the canvas, call clf().

Unit 42

Getting to Know Other Plot Types

In addition to contour and image plots, pyplot supports a variety of more conventional plot types: bar plots, box plots, histograms, pie charts, line plots, log and log-log plots, scatter plots, polar plots, step plots, and so on. The online pyplot gallery[1] offers many examples, and the following table lists many of the pyplot plotting functions.

Plot type	Function
Vertical bar plot	bar()
Horizontal bar plot	barh()
Box plot with "whiskers"	boxplot()
Errorbar plot	errorbar()
Histogram (can be vertical or horizontal)	hist()
Log-log plot	loglog()
Log plot in X	semilogx()
Log plot in Y	semilogy()
Pie chart	pie()
Line plot	plot()
Date plot	plot_dates()
Polar plot	polar()
Scatter plot (size and color of dots can be controlled)	scatter()
Step plot	step()

Table 5—Some pyplot Plot Types

---

1. matplotlib.org/gallery.html

Mastering Embellishments

With pyplot, you can control a lot of aspects of plotting.

You can set and change axes scales ("linear" vs. "log"—logarithmic) with the xscale(scale) and yscale(scale) functions, and you can set and change axes limits with the xlim(xmin, xmax) and ylim(ymin, ymax) functions.

You can set and change font, graph, and background colors, and font and point sizes and styles.

You can also add notes with annotate(), arrows with arrow(), and a legend block with legend(). In general, refer to the pyplot documentation for the complete list of embellishment functions and their arguments, but let's at least add some arrows, notes, and a legend to an already familiar NIAAA graph:

pyplot-legend.py
```
import matplotlib, matplotlib.pyplot as plt
import pickle, pandas as pd

# The NIAAA frame has been pickled before
alco = pickle.load(open("alco.pickle", "rb"))

# Select the right data
BEVERAGE = "Beer"
years = alco.index.levels[1]
states = ("New Hampshire", "Colorado", "Utah")

# Select a good-looking style
plt.xkcd()
matplotlib.style.use("ggplot")

# Plot the charts
for state in states:
    ydata = alco.ix[state][BEVERAGE]
    plt.plot(years, ydata, "-o")
    # Add annotations with arrows
    plt.annotate(s="Peak", xy=(ydata.argmax(), ydata.max()),
                xytext=(ydata.argmax() + 0.5, ydata.max() + 0.1),
                arrowprops={"facecolor": "black", "shrink": 0.2})

# Add labels and legends
plt.ylabel(BEVERAGE + " consumption")
plt.title("And now in xkcd...")
plt.legend(states)

plt.savefig("../images/pyplot-legend-xkcd.pdf")
```

The triple-line plot shown here illustrates the dynamics of beer consumption in three states (in fact, in the most, least, and median beer-drinking states):

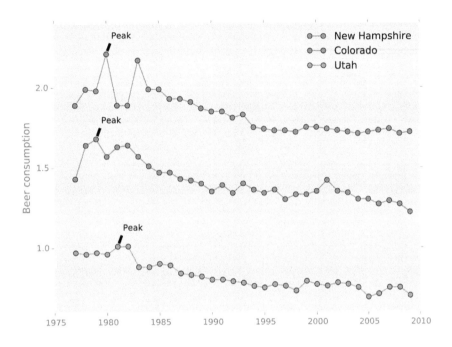

A Note on Unicode

 If your plot contains Unicode (meaning non-Latin) characters, you may need to change the default font before plotting any text by adding a call to matplotlib.rc("font", family="Arial") as the first line of your plotting script.

Finally, you can change the style of a pyplot plot to resemble the popular xkcd[2] web comic with the function xkcd(). (The function affects only the plot elements added after the call to it.) For some reason, we can't save the plots as PostScript files, but everything else works. Nonetheless, you probably should avoid including xkcd-style plots in official presentations because they look as if drawn by a drunk (see the plot on page 142)—unless, of course, the presentation itself is about alcohol consumption.

---

2. xkcd.com

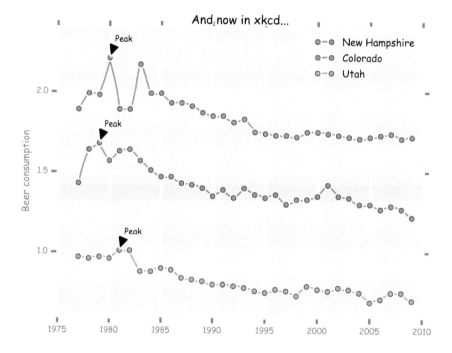

The module pyplot is great on its own. But it's even better when combined with pandas, which we'll look at next.

Unit 44

Plotting with Pandas

Both pandas frames and series support plotting through pyplot. When the plot() function is called without any parameters, it line-plots either the series or all frame columns with labels. If you specify the optional parameters x and y, the function plots column x against column y.

pandas also supports other types of plots via the optional parameter kind. The admissible values of the parameter are "bar" and "barh" for bar plots, "hist" for histograms, "box" for boxplots, "kde" for density plots, "area" for area plots, "scatter" for scatter plots, "hexbin" for hexagonal bin plots, and "pie" for pie charts. All plots allow a variety of embellishments, such as legends, color bars, controllable dot sizes (option s), and colors (option c).

As an example, let's plot wine consumption vs. beer consumption in the state of New Hampshire over the whole NIAAA observation period. We'll color each data point according to the observation year:

```
scatter-plot.py
import matplotlib, matplotlib.pyplot as plt
import pickle, pandas as pd

# The NIAAA frame has been pickled before
alco = pickle.load(open("alco.pickle", "rb"))

# Select a good-locking style
matplotlib.style.use("ggplot")

# Do the scatter plot
STATE = "New Hampshire"
statedata = alco.ix[STATE].reset_index()
statedata.plot.scatter("Beer", "Wine", c="Year", s=100, cmap=plt.cm.autumn)

plt.title("%s: From Beer to Wine in 32 Years" % STATE)
plt.savefig("../images/scatter-plot.pdf")
```

It's not hard to see in the resulting plot on page 144 that in the thirty-two years of observations, the state went through the process of de-beering and en-wineing. Hopefully, the process was not painful and did not also cause de-population.

We'll conclude our plotting tour with the sub-module pandas.tools.plotting. The module has tools for drawing Andrews curves andrews_curves(), lag plots lag_plot(), and autocorrelations autocorrelation_plot()—but, what's more important, pandas.tools.plotting has tools for scatter matrices. A *scatter matrix* is an excellent

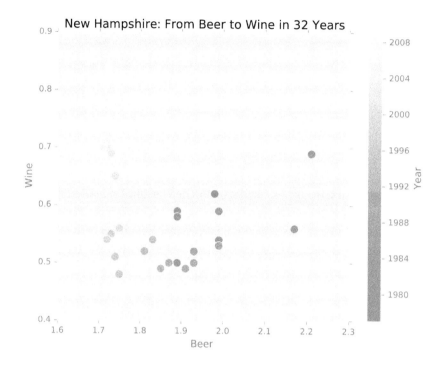

exploratory instrument. It's implemented as the function scatter_matrix(), which displays data histograms for each column in the main diagonal and two-variable scatter plots for each combination of two columns in all other matrix cells.

```
scatter-matrix.py
from pandas.tools.plotting import scatter_matrix
import matplotlib, matplotlib.pyplot as plt
import pickle, pandas as pd

# The NIAAA frame has been pickled before
alco = pickle.load(open("alco.pickle", "rb"))

# Select a good-locking style
matplotlib.style.use("ggplot")

# Plot the scatter matrix
STATE = "New Hampshire"
statedata = alco.ix[STATE].reset_index()
scatter_matrix(statedata[["Wine", "Beer", "Spirits"]],
               s=120, c=statedata["Year"], cmap=plt.cm.autumn)

plt.tight_layout()
plt.savefig("../images/scatter-matrix.pdf")
```

We are again in New Hampshire, exploring the locals' drinking habits, but now all three types and six pairs of beverages in each of the thirty-two recorded years are in the same chart:

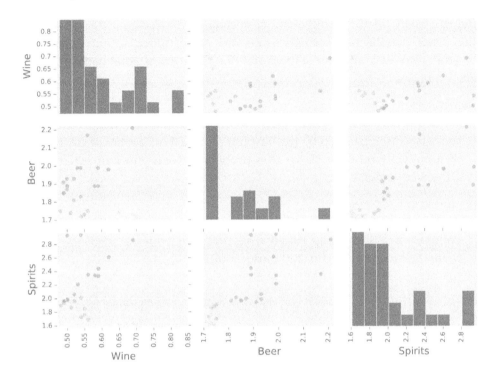

Your Turn

Data plotting (and, in general, data visualization) is not an exercise in futility. They don't say that a picture is worth a thousand words for nothing. In data science, it may be worth millions and perhaps billions of numerical observations. Data visualization furnishes you with powerful tools, both exploratory (for your own eyes) and presentational (for the eyes of your colleagues and data sponsors).

*American Pie**

Write a program that either displays or saves as a PDF file a pie chart of the U.S. states grouped by the first initial. You'll need a list of state names or abbreviations to work on this problem, which you can get from the namesake website.[3]

*Population of California***

Write a program that uses U.S. Census Bureau data[4] to display how the population of California (relative to the total population of the United States) changed between 2001 and 2009.

---

3. www.stateabbreviations.us
4. www.census.gov/popest/data/historical/2000s/vintage_2009/state.html

I shall have to just reduce all that mass of statistics to a few salient facts. There are too many statistics and figures for me.

➤ *Mark Twain, American author and humorist*

CHAPTER 9

Probability and Statistics

Probability theory and statistics study random phenomena, mostly in the form of random samples such as random numbers and random categorical variables.

Probability theory concerns itself with the origin and production of random samples. We draw random samples from appropriate probability distributions and use them to:

- Simulate synthetic raw data for model testing purposes (like we did in Unit 30, *Generating a Synthetic Sine Wave*, on page 80)

- Split raw data into testing and training sets, as explained in Unit 48, *Designing a Predictive Experiment*, on page 158

- Support randomized machine learning algorithms (such as random decision forests, which are covered in Unit 51, *Surviving in Random Decision Forests*, on page 169)

On the other hand, statistics is more about studying properties of already collected random samples. Experimental raw data almost always has an element of uncertainty and unpredictability. We'll use various statistical measures to describe the observations of a dependent variable and possible interactions between dependent and independent variables.

Probability and statistics are great and extensive areas of mathematics. They can't be learned by reading just one chapter in a reference book. In fact, you probably already know some probability and statistics; this unit simply refreshes and summarizes the key concepts. Let's start with some probability theory, continue to mathematical definitions of various statistical measures, and conclude by calculating them in Python.

Reviewing Probability Distributions

A probability distribution assigns a probability to each possible random number (a discrete distribution) or range of random numbers (a continuous distribution). In other words, it tells us if some outcomes are more probable than other outcomes. Commonly encountered probability distributions include the uniform distribution (continuous and discrete), the normal distribution (continuous), and the binomial distribution (discrete).

You can specify a probability distribution by supplying a probability mass function (PMF, for discrete distributions) or probability density function (PDF, for continuous distributions). A PDF describes the relative likelihood a random variable takes on a given value, and a PMF gives the probability that a discrete random variable is exactly equal to some value. The picture shows PDFs (top row) and PMFs (bottom row) of some commonly encountered probability distributions. (Needless to say, the plots were produced with pyplot, as discussed in Unit 41, *Basic Plotting with PyPlot*, on page 136.)

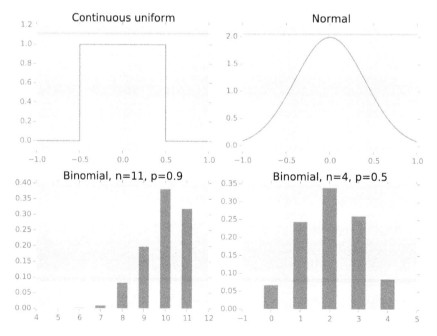

Let's look briefly at the most interesting types of distributions.

Uniform Distribution

The *uniform distribution* is a distribution whereby all outcomes are equally possible. Uniform distributions are often used to represent numeric random variables when all that is known is the range of possible values.

Normal Distribution

The *normal distribution*, also known as a Gaussian distribution or a bell curve, is used to represent real-valued random variables if the mean and standard deviation of their real distribution are known, but not the distribution itself.

Binomial Distribution

The *binomial distribution* is the probability distribution of the number of successes in a sequence of $n>0$ independent binary trials ("coin flips"), each of which yields success ("heads") with probability $0 \leq p \leq 1$. The expected number of successful outcomes is $n \times p$. When $n=1$, the binomial distribution becomes a *Bernoulli distribution*.

A normally distributed random variable is a binomially distributed variable with infinitely many trials and the probability of success of 0.5. In other words, a normally distributed random variable is the cumulative effect on infinitely many equiprobable binary causes.

Long Tails

Some probability distributions (such as Pareto, also known as Zipf or power law) have a "long tail," which is the distribution's PDF that goes far to the right or to the left, resembling a bumpy, long-tailed creature. A long tail means that even the samples that are far from the mean have a non-zero probability and are likely to appear in our data.

Real raw data may or may not fit into any of the theoretical distributions. But even if it doesn't, you can still make important conclusions about it by calculating various statistical measures, which we'll take a look at in the next unit.

Unit 46

Recollecting Statistical Measures

From the point of view of exploratory (non–inference-based) data science, statistics answers four important questions:

Where is the data?

The sample mean is the average of all observations:

$$\overline{x} = \sum x_i / N$$

You can use the sample mean to represent the whole sample when the distribution of data is close to normal ("bell-shaped") and the standard deviation is low.

How broad is the data?

The sample standard deviation is the measure of spread and is calculated as the square root of the average square deviation from the sample mean:

$$s_x = \sqrt{\frac{\sum\left(x_i - \overline{x}\right)^2}{N-1}}$$

High s_x means that the data is widely spread.

How skewed is the data?

Sample skewness is a measure of the asymmetry of the probability distribution. Zero skewness means a symmetric distribution. For a unimodal distribution (a distribution with one mode), negative skewness indicates that the tail on the left side of the probability density function is longer than on the right side.

Are two variables (cor)related?

Sample covariance is a measure of how closely two random variables vary (change) together. The covariance of X with itself is called variance, which is simply s^2 (the square of the standard deviation).

$$q_{xy} = \frac{\sum\left(x_i - \overline{x}\right)\left(y_i - \overline{y}\right)}{N-1}$$

The Pearson correlation coefficient, also known as the correlation coefficient or simply correlation, is a normalized measure of covariance:

$$r_{xy} = \frac{\sum \left(x_i y_i - N \overline{x}\, \overline{y} \right)}{(N-1)s_x s_y}$$

The correlation is always in the range [-1...1]. Take a look at the following table. High correlation means that the variables are correlated. Low correlation means the variables are anti-correlated. Zero correlation means the variables are not linearly related.

	$r \ll 0$	$r = 0$	$r \gg 0$
$p \leq .01$	Significant anti-correlation	No linear relation	Significant correlation
$p > .01$		No linear relation	

Table 6—Types of Linear Relations Between Two Variables

A significant correlation doesn't imply causation. Two variables may be highly correlated or anti-correlated because they are consequences of a common cause (the confounding variable) or just by coincidence. More people drown when days are longer and nights are shorter—but they drown not *because* days are longer, but because in summer, both days are longer and more people go swimming!

Similarly, an insignificant linear correlation doesn't imply a lack of relation between two variables: the relation may be non-linear. When you don't observe a significant linear correlation, don't get desperate. Instead look into other relation models such as clustering, as described in Unit 50, *Grouping Data with K-Means Clustering*, on page 166.

Population and Samples

Though you may not be interested in statistical inference (an art of trying to infer from the sample data what the population might look like), you still need to understand that most of the time data scientists deal not with the entire population of observations, but with a limited-sized sample. All statistical measures itemized in this unit are not true values—they are *estimators*.

When the number of observations in the sample is low, the correlation between two variables may be large—but not necessarily significant. The measure of significance is called a *p-value*. The value of $p \leq .01$ is considered good enough, but the smaller, the better.

We can now move to the Python side and learn how to draw samples from distributions and calculate statistical measures in a Python way.

Doing Stats the Python Way

Python support for random numbers and statistics is scattered across several modules: statistics, numpy.random, pandas, and scipy.stats.

Generating Random Numbers

The numpy.random module has random number generators for all major probability distributions.

Early in this book (on page 6), you learned that data analysis code should be reproducible: anyone should be able to run the same program with the same input data and get the same results. You should always initialize the pseudo random seed with the seed() function. Otherwise, the generators produce different pseudo random sequences with every program run, which may make the results hard or impossible to reproduce.

```
import numpy.random as rnd
rnd.seed(z)
```

The following functions generate uniformly, normally, and binomially distributed integer and real random numbers. All of them return a numpy array of the shape or size (where the shape is a list of dimensions), unless you set the size parameter to None.

```
rnd.uniform(low=0.0, high=1.0, size=None)
rnd.rand(shape) # Same as uniform(0.0, 1.0, None)
rnd.randint(low, high=None, size=None)
rnd.normal(loc=0.0, scale=1.0, size=None)
rnd.randn(shape) # Same as normal(0.0, 1.0, shape)
rnd.binomial(n, p, size=None)
```

The binomial distribution is essential when you need to set up a predictive experiment and split the data into a training set and a testing set (more on predictive experiments in Unit 48, *Designing a Predictive Experiment*, on page 158). Let the relative size of the training set be p, and of the testing set, 1-p. You can prepare a binomial sequence, convert it to a Boolean sequence of True and False values, and select both sets from a pandas frame:

```
selection = rnd.binomial(1, p, size=len(data)).astype(bool)
training = df[selection]
testing = df[-selection]
```

Calculating Statistical Measures

As a quick and dirty solution, the statistics module, which you first encountered on page 35, provides the low-end functions mean() and stdev().

pandas frames and series have functions for calculating correlations and covariances with other series and frames, as well as for calculating all pairwise correlations and covariances between frame columns (but not the p-values) and other statistical measures.

Let's reuse the NIAAA surveillance report you converted into a frame earlier on page 88 to explore the pandas statistics support. (We are not drunkards! We are data scientists: once we've got a good data set, we'll make the best use of it!) Prepare two series and then calculate their correlation, covariance, and skewness:

```
beer_seriesNY = alco.ix['New York']['Beer']
beer_seriesCA = alco.ix['California']['Beer']

beer_seriesNY.corr(beer_seriesCA)
```

⇒ **0.97097785391654789**

```
beer_seriesCA.cov(beer_seriesNY)
```

⇒ **0.017438162878787872**

```
[x.skew() for x in (beer_seriesCA, beer_seriesNY)]
```

⇒ **[0.16457291293004678, 0.32838100586347024]**

We can apply the same functions to frames, too:

```
frameNY = alco.ix['New York']

frameNY.skew()
```

⇒ **Beer   0.328381**
⇒ **Wine   0.127308**
⇒ **Spirits   0.656699**
⇒ **dtype: float64**

```
frameNY.corr() # all pairwise correlations
```

⇒   **Beer   Wine   Spirits**
⇒ **Beer   1.000000 0.470690 0.908969**
⇒ **Wine   0.470690 1.000000 0.611923**
⇒ **Spirits 0.908969 0.611923 1.000000**

```
frameNY.cov() # all pairwise covariances
```

⇒   **Beer   Wine   Spirits**
⇒ **Beer   0.016103 0.002872 0.026020**
⇒ **Wine   0.002872 0.002312 0.006638**
⇒ **Spirits 0.026020 0.006638 0.050888**

The latter two functions return a frame of all pairwise correlations or covariances.

We can also correlate a series and a frame, and a frame and another frame. For example, let's check if there is any correlation between alcohol consumption and state population in New York state using the U.S. Census Bureau data[1] for the time period between 2000 to 2009:

```
# Remove the last two lines: they contain future estimates
pop_seriesNY = pop.ix["New York"][:-2]
# Convert the index from date to integer year
pop_seriesNY.index = pop_seriesNY.index.str.split().str[-1].astype(int)

frameNY.ix[2000:2009].corrwith(pop_seriesNY)
```

```
⇒ Beer       -0.520878
⇒ Wine        0.936026
⇒ Spirits     0.957697
⇒ dtype: float64
```

Notice that the rows in the frame and in the series are arranged in the opposite orders. pandas is smart enough to use the row indexes to match the right rows —which is, of course, the data alignment mechanism in action. (There's more on data alignment on page 109.)

To estimate the significance of the correlation, use the pearsonr() function from the scipy.stats module. This function returns both the correlation and the p-value. However, it is not integrated with pandas frames, and it doesn't support indexing, so it's your job to align the indexes and convert the result back to a frame.

```
from scipy.stats import pearsonr
# Manually align the indexes
pop_sorted = pop_seriesNY.sort_index()
alco_10 = alco.ix['New York'][-10:]
# List comprehension to calculate all correlations and p-values
corrs = [(bev,) + pearsonr(alco_10[bev], pop_sorted)
         for bev in alco_10.columns]
# Convert the list to a frame
pd.DataFrame(corrs, columns=("bev", "r", "p-value")).set_index("bev")
```

```
⇒              r     p-value
⇒ bev
⇒ Beer    -0.520878  0.122646
⇒ Wine     0.936026  0.000068
⇒ Spirits  0.957697  0.000013
```

Note that the p-value for the "beer" correlation is ridiculously high. According to Table 6, *Types of Linear Relations Between Two Variables*, on page 151, we

---

1.   www.census.gov/popest/data/historical/2000s/vintage_2009/state.html

must conclude that it's unlikely that there is a linear relationship between population and beer consumption.

We are now fully equipped to revisit the example from *Cross-Tabulation*, on page 114. Based on the cross-table, we claimed that back in 2009, beer and wine consumptions per capita were probably linearly independent. The Pearson correlation fully confirms our claim:

```
alco2009.corr()
```

```
⇒            Beer      Wine   Spirits
⇒  Beer     1.000000 -0.031560  0.452279
⇒  Wine    -0.031560  1.000000  0.599791
⇒  Spirits  0.452279  0.599791  1.000000
```

The absurdly high p-value of the correlation delivers a *coup de grace* to the alternative hypothesis:

```
pearsonr(alco2009["Wine"], alco2009["Beer"])
```

```
⇒  (-0.031560488300856844, 0.82598481310787297)
```

And the following scatter plot explains why: the points are literally scattered all around the plot in no particular order or pattern.

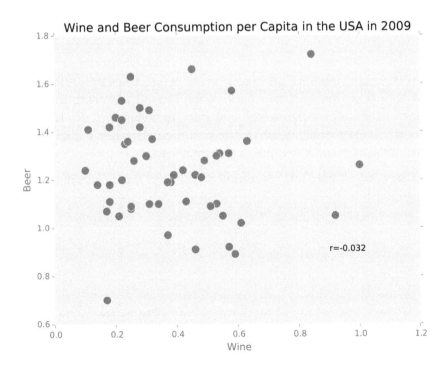

Your Turn

Calling this chapter "Probability and Statistics" was nothing but an act of reckless bravery. It takes a good volume—not mere pages!—to introduce probability theory alone, and another volume for statistics. If this is your first encounter with either discipline and you still want to be a data scientist, you've got to do a lot of reading; *An Introduction to Statistical Learning with Applications in R [JWHT13]* is a good starting point, though you may get confused about the R language used in that book. But even if you're a complete statistical novice, you still can do some interesting projects. Let Python be with you!

*Twenty-First Century S&P 500**

Write a program that reports some basic statistical measures of the closing values of the S&P 500 stock index: the mean, standard deviation, skewness, and correlation between the closing values and trading volume in the twenty-first century. Is the correlation reliable? You can download the historical prices from Yahoo! Finance.[2] Remember that the twenty-first century began on January 1, 2001.

*Network of Nutrients****

The United States Department of Agriculture (USDA) nutrient database[3] contains information about approximately 9,000 food items and 150 constituent nutrients. Let's say that two nutrients are similar if their amounts in all food items are strongly and reliably correlated: the correlation is greater than 0.7 and the p-value is less than 0.01. Write a program that uses the nutrition data in the file NUT_DATA.txt to construct a network of similar nutrients (you may need to revisit Unit 40, *Harnessing Networkx*, on page 127). Each nutrient in the network is a node, and two nodes are connected if two nutrients are similar.

Does the network have any community structure? If it does, what nutrients go together?

---

2.   finance.yahoo.com/q/hp?s=^GSPC+Historical+Prices
3.   www.ars.usda.gov/Services/docs.htm?docid=25700 (document SR28)

On my own farm at Dearborn we do everything by machinery.

> Henry Ford, American industrialist

CHAPTER 10

Machine Learning

Machine learning is a field of study that looks at and constructs algorithms that can learn from and make predictions on experimental data. There are two major classes of machine learning: supervised and unsupervised.

Supervised learning attempts to infer a predictive function from a labeled training data set—a data set where each observation is known to belong to a certain class (the classification is in fact a part of the data set). We'll take a look at linear regression, including logistic regression in Unit 49, *Fitting a Linear Regression*, on page 160, and at random decision forests in Unit 51, *Surviving in Random Decision Forests*, on page 169. (Due to the limited scope of this book, we will sadly ignore naive Bayes classification, support vector machines, linear discriminant analysis, and neural networks.)

Unsupervised learning tries to find hidden structure in unlabeled data. Some of the most popular unsupervised techniques are k-means clustering (discussed in Unit 50, *Grouping Data with K-Means Clustering*, on page 166) and community detection (previously discussed on page 132). Hierarchical clustering and principal component analysis are also unsupervised algorithms—but we have no time and space to talk about them here.

Both types of machine learning tools can be used for exploratory and predictive data analysis. You'll find the Python implementations of the tools in the SciKit-Learn module and its sub-modules. If your goal is to predict something that you haven't seen rather than to explain something you see, you first must set up a predictive experiment.

Designing a Predictive Experiment

Predictive data analysis is a real scientific experiment, and it must be organized as such. You cannot just claim that your data mode predicts something —an important part of an experiment is the assessment and validation of its predictive power.

To build, assess, and validate a model, follow these four steps:

1. Split the input data into training and testing sets (the recommended split ratio is 70:30). Then set the testing data aside and never use it for preparing the data model.

2. Build a data model using only the training data.

3. Apply the new model to the testing data.

4. Evaluate the model quality with the confusion matrix or some other quality assurance tool. If the model passes the test, it is adequate. Otherwise, repeat the last three steps.

A binary confusion matrix is a table with two rows and two columns that allows someone to assess the accuracy of a binary predictive model (a model that predicts whether some property holds or does not hold), as illustrated by the following table:

Classified as		
Positive	*Negative*	Really is
True positive (TP)	False negative (FN)	*Positive*
False positive (FP)	True negative (TN)	*Negative*

Table 7—Binary Confusion Matrix

We assume that we know whether or not any item in the testing set has the predicted property, and we used the model to predict the property for each item, too. (Clearly, this assumption holds only for supervised learning models!) TP refers to the number of items for which the model correctly predicted the property as present (true positive); TN refers to the number of items for which the model correctly predicted the property as absent (true negative); FP refers to the number of items for which the model incorrectly predicted the property as present (false positive); and FN refers to the number of items for which the model incorrectly predicted the property as absent (false negative).

Other Machine Learning Techniques

 Other supervised and unsupervised machine learning techniques include naive Bayes classification, support vector machines (SVN), linear discriminant analysis (LDA), and neural networks. Some of them are provided by SciKit-Learn.

Quantitative measures are defined to summarize the content of the matrix:

- *Accuracy* is the proportion of correctly classified items:

$$\text{accuracy} = \frac{TP + TN}{TP + TN + FP + FN}$$

At the very least, your predictive model must have high accuracy. If it doesn't, it's not even accurate!

- *Precision* is the proportion of true positives to all classified positives:

$$\text{precision} = \frac{TP}{TP + FP}$$

- *Sensitivity* (or *recall*) is the proportion of true positives to all real positives:

$$\text{sensitivity} = \frac{TP}{TP + FN}$$

Sensitivity explains how good the model is in recognizing the observed property. If true positives are rare (say, cancer cases among the general population), the model has to be sensitive to be useful.

- *Specificity* is the proportion of true negatives to all real negatives:

$$\text{specificity} = \frac{TN}{TN + FP}$$

High specificity means that the model is good in capturing the absence of the property.

Many statistical models have either high sensitivity but low specificity, or low sensitivity but high specificity, depending on the model parameters. Choose the parameters based on which measure is more important to you. If a predictor has both poor specificity and sensitivity, you can invert it to become a good predictor.

If the predicted value is not binary (say, categorical or continuous), you must use other quality control tools, some of which you'll learn in the rest of this chapter.

Unit 49

Fitting a Linear Regression

Linear regression is a form of predictive statistical modeling that aims at explaining all or some of a variable's variance using a linear model. It's a supervised modeling technique: you must train ("fit") the model before using it for prediction.

Ordinary Least Square Regression

Ordinary least squares (OLS) regression relates independent variables (predictors) and dependent variables (predicted value). The model treats the predicted value $reg(x_i)$ as a linear combination of predictors x_i. The differences between the real y_i and predicted values are called residuals. In the case of a perfect fit, all residuals are zero. The sum of possibly weighted (with weights $w_i > 0$) squared residuals, SSR, determines the quality of fit. Training the model means minimizing the SSR:

$$SSR = \sum_{i}^{N} (y_i - reg(x_i))^2 w_i^2 \rightarrow \min$$

Another measure of quality of fit is the model *score*, also known as R^2. The score $0 \leq R^2 \leq 1$ shows how much variance the fitted model explains. In the case of a perfect fit, $R^2 = 1$. In the case of a very bad fit, $R^2 \approx 0$.

The constructor LinearRegression() from the sklearn.linear_model module creates an OLS regression object.

The fit() function takes a 1×n matrix of predictors. If the model has one independent variable and the predictors form a vector, slicing with the numpy.newaxis object is used to create another dimension. The true values of the dependent variable are passed as a one-dimensional vector. (If you want to predict more than one property, you must build and fit more than one model.)

After fitting, you can use the regression object for calculating the predicted values (the function predict()) and checking the fit score (the function score()). The attributes coef_ and intercept_ contain the values of the regression coefficients and the intercept after the fit.

The following example uses the historical S&P 500 closing prices from Yahoo! Finance[1] to build, fit, and evaluate a linear regression model. It assumes that the data has been previously saved as sapXXI.csv.

Begin by importing all necessary modules and loading the S&P 500 data:

sap-linregr.py
```python
import numpy, pandas as pd
import matplotlib, matplotlib.pyplot as plt
import sklearn.linear_model as lm

# Get the data
sap = pd.read_csv("sapXXI.csv").set_index("Date")
```

You can see by visually exploring the closing prices that their behavior in general is far from linear, but there is a nice, almost linear, fragment that starts on January 1, 2009 and extends to the end of the data set. You'll use only this fragment for model fitting. Unfortunately, SciKit-Learn does not support dates directly. Therefore, you must convert them to ordinal numbers—days —and then create, fit, and evaluate the linear regression model, and calculate the predicted S&P 500 values. The model score is 0.95, which is not so bad!

sap-linregr.py
```python
# Select a "linearly looking" part
sap.index = pd.to_datetime(sap.index)
sap_linear = sap.ix[sap.index > pd.to_datetime('2009-01-01')]

# Prepare the model and fit it
olm = lm.LinearRegression()
X = numpy.array([x.toordinal() for x in sap_linear.index])[:, numpy.newaxis]
y = sap_linear['Close']
olm.fit(X, y)

# Predict values
yp = [olm.predict(x.toordinal())[0] for x in sap_linear.index]

# Evaluate the model
olm_score = olm.score(X, y)
```

Finally, the code draws the original data set, the predicted line, and even the model score. The result is shown in the image on page 162.

---

1. finance.yahoo.com/q/hp?s=^GSPC+Historical+Prices

```
sap-linregr.py
# Select a nice plotting style
matplotlib.style.use("ggplot")

# Plot both data sets
plt.plot(sap_linear.index, y)
plt.plot(sap_linear.index, yp)

# Add decorations
plt.title("OLS Regression")
plt.xlabel("Year")
plt.ylabel("S&P 500 (closing)")
plt.legend(["Actual", "Predicted"], loc="lower right")
plt.annotate("Score=%.3f" % olm_score,
             xy=(pd.to_datetime('2010-06-01'), 1900))

plt.savefig("../images/sap-linregr.pdf")
```

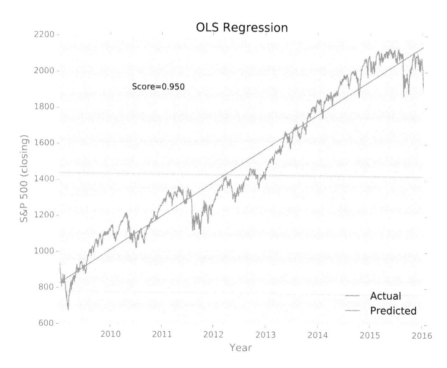

Unfortunately, SciKit-Learn does not calculate the p-value of the fit. It is not possible to tell if the fit is significant or not.

If you want to add some non-linear predictors (for example, squares, square roots, and logarithms) or even combinations of the original predictors to the model, simply treat these functions and combinations as new independent variables.

Ridge Regression

If two or more predictors are highly correlated (the case of so-called *collinearity*), fitting an OLS regression may produce very large coefficients. You can impose a penalty to restrict the uncontrollable growth of the regression coefficients. Ridge regression, a generalized linear model, uses α, a complexity parameter, to suppress the coefficients. This procedure is called model *regularization*:

$$SSR_{gen} = \sum_i^N (y_i - reg(x_i))^2 w_i^2 + \alpha \sum_i^N coeff_i^2 \rightarrow min$$

When α=0, ridge regression becomes OLS regression. When α is high, the penalty is high; the model fitting results in lower coefficients, but the fitted model potentially gets worse.

The function Ridge() creates a ridge regression object. It takes α as the parameter. Once you create the object, you can use it just like you used the OLS regression:

```
regr = lm.Ridge(alpha=.5)
regr.fit(X, y)
«...»
```

Logistic (Logit) Regression

Despite its name, logistic, or logit, regression is not a regression—it is a tool for binary classification. It uses a generalized logistic function (the extension of a logistic function, which is also known as an s-curve or a sigmoid, as shown in the figure on page 164). The generalized logistic function is characterized by the lower and upper asymptotes, the x value of the sigmoid's midpoint, and the steepness of the curve.

The function LogisticRegression() creates an instance of a logistic regression object. It takes several optional parameters, of which the most important is C.

The parameter C is the inverse regularization (the inverse of α for ridge regression). For the results of the classification to make sense, it's often best to make it at least 20. The default value of C=1.0 is unacceptable for many practical purposes.

The dependent variable y can be either integer, Boolean, or string.

sklearn.linear_model implements the classification through the predict() function. Unlike the linear regression models (OLS and ridge), the prediction results of the logit regression model are usually more valuable than the model coefficients coef_ and the intercept intercept_.

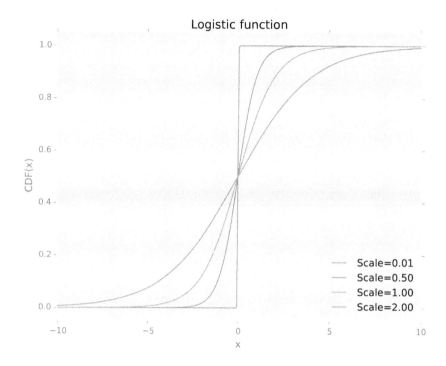

In the next example, you'll use anonymized quiz grades from an introductory computer science class of forty-three students (available in the file grades.csv) to illustrate logistic regression. Let's see if the results of the first two quizzes (out of ten) can predict the final letter grade of a student or at least whether the grade will be satisfactory (a "C" or above) or unsatisfactory:

logit-example.py

```python
import pandas as pd
from sklearn.metrics import confusion_matrix
import sklearn.linear_model as lm

# Initialize the regression tool
clf = lm.LogisticRegression(C=10.0)

# Read the data sheet, quantize letter grades
grades = pd.read_table("grades.csv")
labels = ('F', 'D', 'C', 'B', 'A')
grades["Letter"] = pd.cut(grades["Final score"], [0, 60, 70, 80, 90, 100],
                          labels=labels)
X = grades[["Quiz 1", "Quiz 2"]]

# Fit the model, display the score and the confusion matrix
clf.fit(X, grades["Letter"])
print("Score=%.3f" % clf.score(X, grades["Letter"]))
cm = confusion_matrix(clf.predict(X), grades["Letter"])
```

```
print(pd.DataFrame(cm, columns=labels, index=labels))
```

⇒ **Score=0.535**
⇒   **F**   **D** **C** **B** **A**
⇒ **F** 0   0 0 0 0
⇒ **D** 2 16 6 4 1
⇒ **C** 0   1 6 2 2
⇒ **B** 0   0 0 1 2
⇒ **A** 0   0 0 0 0

We used the confusion_matrix() function from the module sklearn.metrics to calculate the confusion matrix (refer to Table 7, *Binary Confusion Matrix*, on page 158). The model score doesn't look excitingly accurate: the model was able to predict only ≈54% of all grades correctly. However, the confusion matrix has almost all non-zero entries either on the main diagonal (where they belong) or on its neighbors. This means that the model is either accurate or makes a mistake of ±1 letter step. For most practical applications, this "extended" accuracy (84%) is quite sufficient.

Grouping Data with K-Means Clustering

Clustering is an unsupervised machine learning technique. You do not need to (and cannot!) train the model.

The goal of clustering is to collect samples (represented as n-dimensional vectors of real numbers) into disjoint compact groups with good internal proximity. For clustering to work, the vector dimensions must have reasonably compatible ranges. If the range of one dimension is much higher or much lower than the ranges of the other dimensions, you should scale the variables that are "too tall" or "too short" before clustering.

The k-means clustering aggregates samples into k clusters (hence the name) according to the following algorithm:

1. Randomly choose k vectors as the initial centroids (the vectors don't have to be samples from the data set).

2. Assign each sample to the closest centroid.

3. Recalculate centroid positions.

4. Repeat steps 2–3 until the centroids don't move.

The module sklearn.cluster implements the algorithm through the object KMeans, which has the functions fit() for actual clustering, predict() for assigning new samples to pre-computed clusters, and fit_predict() for clustering and labeling at the same time.

The module sklearn.preprocessing has the function scale() for scaling the variables. The function subtracts the minimum value from each dimensional variable and divides the variable by the range, thus mapping it to the [0...1] segment.

The attributes cluster_centers_ and labels_ contain the vectors describing the final centroids, and numeric labels assigned to each sample cluster. The latter labels don't reflect the purpose and composition of the clusters. To assign meaningful labels to clusters, you can do one of the following:

- Use human intelligence (look into the samples and come up with a generalized label).

- Use crowdsourcing (for example, Amazon MTurk workers).

- Generate labels from the data (for example, designate one of the attributes of the most prominent sample as the cluster label).

In *Calculating Statistical Measures*, on page 153, we tried to make sense out of wine and beer consumption in the United States in 2009, and we came to a counterproductive conclusion that the two were not linearly related. Let's give the noble drinks another chance—now through clustering. The process and its results are shown in the following listing:

```
clusters.py
import matplotlib, matplotlib.pyplot as plt
import pickle, pandas as pd
import sklearn.cluster, sklearn.preprocessing

# The NIAAA frame has been pickled before
alco2009 = pickle.load(open("alco2009.pickle", "rb"))
# States" abbreviations
states = pd.read_csv("states.csv",
                     names=("State", "Standard", "Postal", "Capital"))
columns = ["Wine", "Beer"]
# Initialize the clustering object, fit the model
kmeans = sklearn.cluster.KMeans(n_clusters=9)
kmeans.fit(alco2009[columns])
alco2009["Clusters"] = kmeans.labels_
centers = pd.DataFrame(kmeans.cluster_centers_, columns=columns)

# Select a good-looking style
matplotlib.style.use("ggplot")

# Plot the states and cluster centroids
ax = alco2009.plot.scatter(columns[0], columns[1], c="Clusters",
                           cmap=plt.cm.Accent, s=100)
centers.plot.scatter(columns[0], columns[1], color="red", marker="+",
                     s=200, ax=ax)

# Add state abbreviations as annotations
def add_abbr(state):
    _ = ax.annotate(state["Postal"], state[columns], xytext=(1, 5),
                    textcoords="offset points", size=8,
                    color="darkslategrey")

alco2009withStates = pd.concat([alco2009, states.set_index("State")],
                               axis=1)
alco2009withStates.apply(add_abbr, axis=1)

# Add the title, save the plot
plt.title("US States Clustered by Alcohol Consumption")
plt.savefig("../images/clusters.pdf")
```

Note that the KMeans() function always produces eight clusters, unless you pass the n_clusters parameter. It's up to you and your intuition to choose the number of clusters.

Let's plot both the original data (filled circles, labeled by state name abbreviations) and the cluster centroids (crosses) in the same chart, as shown here:

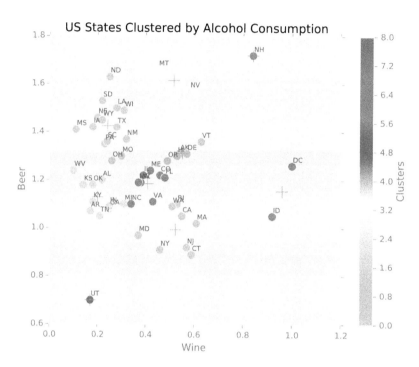

KMeans() did a good job recognizing the clusters (such as the moderately-drinking-both-wine-and-beer Northeast). Label placement leaves much to be desired, but this topic is outside of the scope of this book.

Voronoi Cells

 The k-means clustering algorithm partitions the independent variables space into Voronoi cells—regions of points that are closer to one seed (data point) than to any other seed.

Unit 51

Surviving in Random Decision Forests

A decision tree is a supervised machine learning tool. It uses a tree-style graph where each node contains a test on a certain data set attribute, and the branches incident to the node correspond to the outcomes of the test. If you use trees, you have to train them before use. Training consists of presenting various predictors and corresponding labels (features) to the tree and adjusting the node test conditions accordingly. (Surely, you don't do training by hand!)

A random decision forest regressor uses a number (an *ensemble*) of classifying decision trees on various sub-samples of the data set and averages the predictions to improve accuracy. The module sklearn.ensemble provides the constructor RandomForestRegressor(). The regressor object has the functions fit(), predict(), and so on, which have consistent syntax and semantics with the other regressors that you've seen in this chapter so far.

We'll use the data set of Hedonic Prices of Census Tracts in the Boston Area,[2] first published by D. Harrison and D. Rubinfeld in 1978, to practice random decision forests. The data set provides 506 observations of median values of residential houses (mv, the label in your experiment) and fourteen other variables (predictors).

rfr.py
```
from sklearn.ensemble import RandomForestRegressor
import pandas as pd, numpy.random as rnd
import matplotlib, matplotlib.pyplot as plt

# Read the data, prepare two random complementary data sets
hed = pd.read_csv('Hedonic.csv')
selection = rnd.binomial(1, 0.7, size=len(hed)).astype(bool)
training = hed[selection]
testing = hed[-selection]

# Create a regressor and predictor sets
rfr = RandomForestRegressor()
predictors_tra = training.ix[:, "crim" : "lstat"]
predictors_tst = testing.ix[:, "crim" : "lstat"]

# Fit the model
feature = "mv"
rfr.fit(predictors_tra, training[feature])
```
❶

---

2.   rcom.univie.ac.at/mirrors/lib.stat.cmu.edu/datasets/boston

```
# Select a good-locking style
matplotlib.style.use("ggplot")

# Plot the prediction results
plt.scatter(training[feature], rfr.predict(predictors_tra), c="green",
            s=50)
plt.scatter(testing[feature], rfr.predict(predictors_tst), c="red")
plt.legend(["Training data", "Testing data"], loc="upper left")
plt.plot(training[feature], training[feature], c="blue")
plt.title("Hedonic Prices of Census Tracts in the Boston Area")
plt.xlabel("Actual value")
plt.ylabel("Predicted value")
plt.savefig("../images/rfr.pdf")
```

We fit the predictor using the training data set (randomly chosen from the complete data set) at ❶ and then test both on the training set (at ❷) and the testing set that was not used for fitting (at ❸). The predicted feature mv is not discrete, which precludes us from using a confusion matrix to assess the model quality. Instead, we resort to visual inspection, which suggests that the quality of prediction on both sets is at least fair. Looks like the model is reasonably accurate and not over-fitted:

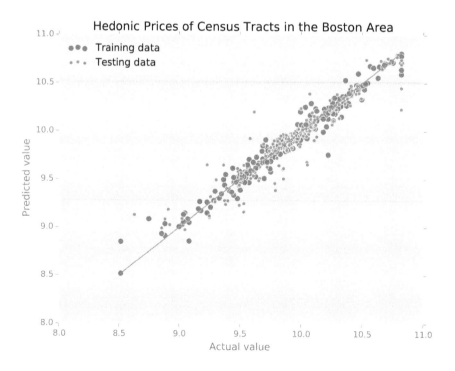

Your Turn

In this chapter, you've only touched the tip of the machine learning iceberg. (If "traditional" science is to be trusted, two-thirds of a typical iceberg is hidden underwater.) However, you have sufficiently powerful tools and knowledge for supervised and unsupervised data processing. You can set up both descriptive (regression and classification) and predictive data science experiments, somewhat assess their validity, and make non-trivial conclusions.

Congratulations! You are almost a data scientist now. (But you still need to complete the remaining projects.)

MOSN Clusters[*]

Write a program that clusters massive online social networking sites by the number of registered users and global Alexa page ranking.[3] Because site ranks and sizes vary in a broad range, use logarithmic scale both for clustering and for presentation.

Piecewise-Linear S&P 500[**]

Write a program that takes the historical S&P 500 closing prices in the twenty-first century from Yahoo! Finance[4] and represent each year's worth of observations as an OLS regression model. If a model score is not adequate (0.95 or below), the program should split the time interval in two halves and proceed recursively until either the OLS model score exceeds 0.95 or the interval is shorter than one week. The program should then plot the original S&P 500 prices and the predicted values from the OLS models in one chart.

Subway Predictor[***]

Develop a program that predicts whether a city has a subway system. Your program may need to look at the population, population density, budget size, weather conditions, income tax levels, and other variables. Some of them may be easily available online, some not. Use logistic regression and random decision forest and choose the method that performs best.

---

3. en.wikipedia.org/wiki/List_of_social_networking_websites
4. finance.yahoo.com/q/hp?s=^GSPC+Historical+Prices

When you have chosen a section of the book which particularly appeals to you, begin your actual study by reading the phrases aloud.

Grenville Kleiser, North American author

APPENDIX 1

Further Reading

If you get to this page, you already know that this book doesn't provide any in-depth coverage of the material and assumes that you mostly know what to do but are not sure how. Here I refer you to several excellent and somewhat overlapping books that provide more details on specific topics.

If you're not familiar with data science at all and either already know the R language or at least don't mind learning it, look at *An Introduction to Statistical Learning with Applications in R [JWHT13]* and *Practical Data Science with R [ZM14]*. The former book is statistical with elements of practical programming, and the latter is practical with elements of statistics, which makes them a good bundle. Another book, *The Elements of Data Analytic Style [Lee15]*, goes over different data model types, writing reports, creating support figures, and writing reproducible code.

Python for Data Analysis [McK12], the classical pandas book by Wes McKinney, the pandas creator himself, contains everything you want to know about pandas and numpy, including financial time series analysis. The book goes over a lot of case studies in great detail.

Natural Language Processing with Python [BKL09] doubles as a Python tutorial and a complete NLP solution. It goes far beyond the modest text normalization and word counting toward text classification, sentence structure analysis, and semantic analysis—and assumes you know no Python and are willing to grab an official free copy online![1]

The social web is an enormous and exponentially expanding repository of raw data. *Mining the Social Web [Rus11]* scrutinizes application programming interfaces (APIs) that allow you to use Unix-style mailboxes, Twitter, LinkedIn, Google Buzz, and Facebook. It has a decent overview of most vital natural

---

1. www.nltk.org/book

language processing tasks. Unfortunately, despite having been published only a few years ago, the book is already mostly obsolete: some APIs have changed, and some social network projects (such as Google Buzz) have been terminated for good.

MySQL Crash Course [For05] is exactly what it claims to be: a comprehensive crash course on how to set up, maintain, and operate relational databases. The book doesn't address any APIs, either in Python or in any other language.

As of the time of this writing, there is no Python-related book on network analysis. *Network Analysis: Methodological Foundations [BE05]* is not intended for computer programmers and, in fact, is quite theoretical. *Social Network Analysis [KY07]* is much more accessible to the practitioners who prefer to stay away from theorems, proofs, and skyscraper-tall formulas. Despite the name, the book is a good introduction to networks in general, not just social networks.

Finally, *Data Science from Scratch [Gru15]* is a somewhat expanded version of this book. It features expanded coverage of statistics and machine learning and would be the most natural next book to read.

In many cases we should never reason out the right solution of a problem; we lack the data.

⸻ *Durant Drake, North American ethics researcher*

Solutions to Single-Star Projects

This appendix provides sample solutions to select (single-star) projects. The suggested solutions are implemented in the most "Pythonic" way. If your own solutions are different, don't get desperate! Just like there is always more than one way to write about love and death, there is always more than one way to solve a programming problem.

Hello, World!

Write a program that outputs "Hello, World!" (less the quotes) on the Python command line (original problem on page 8).

solution-hello.py
```python
# Honor the tradition
print("Hello, World!")
```

Word Frequency Counter

Write a program that downloads a web page requested by the user, and reports up to ten most frequently used words. The program should treat all words as case-insensitive. For the purpose of this exercise, assume that a word is described by the regular expression r"\w+" (original problem on page 28).

solution-counter.py
```python
import urllib.request, re
from collections import Counter

# Talk to the user and the Internet
url = input("Enter the URL: ")
try:
    page = urllib.request.urlopen(url)
except:
    print("Cannot open %s" % url)
    quit()

# Read and partially normalize the page
```

```
doc = page.read().decode().lower()

# Split the text into words
words = re.findall(r"\w+", doc)

# Build a counter and report the answer
print(Counter(words).most_common(10))
```

Broken Link Detector

Write a program that, given a URL of a web page, reports the names and destinations of broken links in the page. For the purpose of this exercise, a link is broken if an attempt to open it with urllib.request.urlopen() fails (original problem on page 44).

```
solution-broken_link.py
import urllib.request, urllib.parse
import bs4 as BeautifulSoup

# Talk to the user and the Internet
base = input("Enter the URL: ")
try:
    page = urllib.request.urlopen(base)
except:
    print("Cannot open %s" % base)
    quit()

# Cook the soup
soup = BeautifulSoup.BeautifulSoup(page)

# Extract the links as (name, url) tuples
links = [(link.string, link["href"])
        for link in soup.find_all("a")
        if link.has_attr("href")]

# Try to open each link
broken = False
for name, url in links:
    # Combine the base and the link destinatuon
    dest = urllib.parse.urljoin(base, url)
    try:
        page = urllib.request.urlopen(dest)
        page.close()
    except:
        print("Link \"%s\" to \"%s\" is probably broken." % (name, dest))
        broken = True

# Good news!
if not broken:
    print("Page %s does not seem to have broken links." % base)
```

MySQL File Indexer

Write a Python program that, for each word in a given file, records the word itself (not the stem!), its ordinal number in the file (starting from 1), and the part-of-speech marker in a MySQL database. Use NLTK WordPunctTokenizer (introduced on page 41) to recognize words. Assume that words are short enough to fit in the TINYTEXT MySQL data type. Design the database schema, create all necessary tables, and play with them via the command-line interface before starting any Python coding (original problem on page 61).

The solution consists of two files: a MySQL script that sets up the table, and a Python program that performs the actual indexing.

solution-mysql_indexer.sql
```
CREATE TABLE IF NOT EXISTS indexer(id INT PRIMARY KEY AUTO_INCREMENT,
                                   ts TIMESTAMP,
                                   word TINYTEXT,
                                   position INT,
                                   pos VARCHAR(8));
```

solution-mysql_indexer.py
```python
import nltk, pymysql

infilename = input("Enter the name of the file to index: ")

# Change this line to match your MySQL server settings
conn = pymysql.connect(user="dsuser", passwd="badpassw0rd", db="dsbd")
cur = conn.cursor()

QUERY = "INSERT INTO indexer (word,position,pos) VALUES "
wpt = nltk.WordPunctTokenizer()

offset = 1
with open(infilename) as infile:
    # Process the text incrementally, one line at a time
    # A word cannot span across lines, anyway!
    for text in infile:
        # Tokenize and add POS tags
        pieces = enumerate(nltk.pos_tag(wpt.tokenize(text)))

        # Create a query; do not forget to escape the words!
        words = ["(\"%s\",%d,\"%s\")" % (conn.escape_string(w),
                                         i + offset,
                                         conn.escape_string(pos))
                 for (i, (w, pos)) in pieces]

        # Execute the query
        if words:
            cur.execute(QUERY + ','.join(words))

            # Advance the word pointer
            offset += len(words)
# Commit the changes
conn.commit()
conn.close()
```

Array Differentiator

Partial sums are a rough equivalent of an integral. In fact, calculus defines an integral as an infinite sum of infinitesimal elements. Partial differences arr_{i+1}-arr_i are a rough equivalent of a derivative. numpy doesn't provide a tool for calculating partial array differences. Write a program that, given an array arr, calculates the partial differences of the array items. Assume that the array is numerical (original problem on page 82).

solution-difference.py
```python
import numpy as np

# Some synthetic data for testing
array = np.random.binomial(5, 0.5, size=100)

# The partial differences: slicing & broadcasting!
diff = array[1:] - array[:-1]
```

Lynx Trappings

Write a program that uses the annual Canadian lynx trappings data[1] and reports total lynx trappings by decade (ten years), sorted in the reverse order (most "productive" decade first). The program should download the data file into the cache directory—but only if the file is not in the cache yet. If the directory does not exist, it will be created. The program should save the results into a CSV file in the directory doc. If the directory doesn't exist, it will be created (original problem on page 119).

solution-lynx.py
```python
import os, pandas as pd
import urllib.request

# Some "constants"
SRC_HOST = "https://vincentarelbundock.github.io"
FILE = "/lynx.csv"
SRC_NAME = SRC_HOST + "/Rdatasets/csv/datasets" + FILE
CACHE = "cache"
DOC = "doc"

# Prepare the directories, if needed
if not os.path.isdir(CACHE):
    os.mkdir(CACHE)
if not os.path.isdir(DOC):
    os.mkdir(DOC)

# Check if the file is cached; cache it if it's not
if not os.path.isfile(CACHE + FILE):
    try:
        src = urllib.request.urlopen(SRC_NAME)
        lynx = pd.read_csv(src)
```

---

1. vincentarelbundock.github.io/Rdatasets/csv/datasets/lynx.csv

```
    except:
        print("Cannot access %f." % SRC_NAME)
        quit()
    # Create a data frame
    lynx.to_csv(CACHE + FILE)
else:
    lynx = pd.read_csv(CACHE + FILE)

# Add the "decade" column
lynx["decade"] = (lynx['time'] / 10).round() * 10

# Aggregate and sort
by_decade = lynx.groupby("decade").sum()
by_decade = by_decade.sort_values(by="lynx", ascending=False)

# Save the results
by_decade["lynx"].to_csv(DOC + FILE)
```

Centrality Correlations

Download a social network graph of select Epinions.com users from the Stanford Large Network Dataset Collection,[2] and extract the tenth largest community. Write a program that calculates and displays pairwise correlations between all network centrality measures mentioned in Chapter 7, *Working with Network Data*, on page 121; you can also add a clustering coefficient for more fun (original problem on page 134). I suggest that you store all centralities in a pandas data frame. You may need to read about how to calculate correlations in pandas in *Calculating Statistical Measures*, on page 153.

Are any pairs of centralities really strongly correlated?

```
solution-centrality.py
import networkx as nx, community
import pandas as pd

# Import the network
G = nx.read_adjlist(open("soc-Epinions1.txt", "rb"))

# Extract community structure and save it as a data series
partition = pd.Series(community.best_partition(G))

# Find the index of the 10th largest community
top10 = partition.value_counts().index[9]

# Extract the 10th largest community
# Remember that node labels are strings!
subgraph = partition[partition == top10].index.values.astype('str')
F = G.subgraph(subgraph)

# Calculate the network measures
df = pd.DataFrame()
df["degree"] = pd.Series(nx.degree_centrality(F))
```

---

2.   snap.stanford.edu/data/soc-Epinions1.html

```
df["closeness"] = pd.Series(nx.closeness_centrality(F))
df["betweenness"] = pd.Series(nx.betweenness_centrality(F))
df["eigenvector"] = pd.Series(nx.eigenvector_centrality(F))
df["clustering"] = pd.Series(nx.clustering(F))

# Calculate the correlations
print(df.corr())
```

```
⇒                degree   closeness  betweenness  eigenvector  clustering
⇒   degree       1.000000   0.247377     0.871812     0.738836    0.100259
⇒   closeness     0.247377   1.000000     0.169449     0.547228    0.024052
⇒   betweenness   0.871812   0.169449     1.000000     0.527290   -0.015759
⇒   eigenvector   0.738836   0.547228     0.527290     1.000000    0.143070
⇒   clustering    0.100259   0.024052    -0.015759     0.143070    1.000000
```

The degree centrality is strongly linearly correlated with the betweenness and eigenvector centralities.

American Pie

Write a program that either displays or saves as a PDF file a pie chart of the U.S. states grouped by the first initial. You'll need a list of state names or abbreviations to work on this problem. You can get it from the namesake website[3] (original problem on page 146).

```
solution-states_pie.py
import pandas as pd
import matplotlib, matplotlib.pyplot as plt

def initial(word):
    return word[0]

# Read the state names (use whatever source you like!)
states = pd.read_csv("states.csv",
                names=("State", "Standard", "Postal", "Capital"))

# Select a good-locking style
matplotlib.style.use("ggplot")

# Plotting
plt.axes(aspect=1)
states.set_index('Postal').groupby(initial).count()['Standard'].plot.pie()
plt.title("States by the First Initial")
plt.ylabel("")

plt.savefig("../images/states-pie.pdf")
```

The resulting pie chart is shown here:

---

3.   www.stateabbreviations.us

States by the First Initial

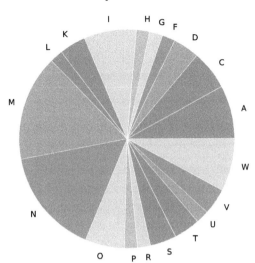

Twenty-First Century S&P 500

Write a program that reports some basic statistical measures of the closing values of the S&P 500 stock index: the mean, standard deviation, skewness, and correlation between the closing values and trading volume in the twenty-first century. Is the correlation reliable? You can download the historical prices from Yahoo! Finance.[4] Remember that the twenty-first century began on January 1, 2001 (original problem on page 156).

Your new downloaded data will be different from the data I used in this example, and your answers may differ from mine.

```
solution-sap.py
import pandas as pd
from scipy.stats import pearsonr

# Read the data
sap = pd.read_csv("sapXXI.csv").set_index("Date")

# Calculate and report all stats
print("Mean:", sap["Close"].mean())
print("Standard deviation:", sap["Close"].std())
print("Skewness:", sap["Close"].skew())
print("Correlation:\n", sap[["Close", "Volume"]].corr())
_, p = pearsonr(sap["Close"], sap["Volume"])
```

---

4. finance.yahoo.com/q/hp?s=^GSPC+Historical+Prices

```
    print("p-value:", p)
```

⇒ **Mean: 1326.35890044**
⇒ **Standard deviation: 332.784759688**
⇒ **Skewness: 0.858098114571**
⇒ **Correlation:**
⇒   **Close   Volume**
⇒ **Close 1.000000 0.103846**
⇒ **Volume 0.103846 1.000000**
⇒ **p-value: 1.5301705092e-10**

The correlation is very reliable—but very insignificant.

MOSN Clusters

Write a program that clusters massive online social networking (MOSN) sites by the number of registered users and global Alexa page ranking.[5] Because site ranks and sizes vary in a broad range, use logarithmic scale both for clustering and for presentation (original problem on page 171).

```
solution-mosn.py
import pandas as pd, numpy as np
import sklearn.cluster, sklearn.preprocessing
import matplotlib, matplotlib.pyplot as plt

# Read the data
mosn = pd.read_csv('mosn.csv', thousands=',',
                   names=('Name', 'Description', 'Date', 'Registered Users',
                          'Registration', 'Alexa Rank'))
columns = ['Registered Users', 'Alexa Rank']

# Eliminate rows with missing data and zeros
good = mosn[np.log(mosn[columns]).notnull().all(axis=1)].copy()

# Do clustering
kmeans = sklearn.cluster.KMeans()
kmeans.fit(np.log(good[columns]))
good["Clusters"] = kmeans.labels_

# Which one is the Facebook?
fb = good.set_index('Name').ix['Facebook']['Clusters']

# Select a good-locking style
matplotlib.style.use("ggplot")

# Display the results
ax = good.plot.scatter(columns[0], columns[1], c="Clusters",
                       cmap=plt.cm.Accent, s=100)
plt.title("Massive online social networking sites")
plt.xscale("log")
plt.yscale("log")

# Annotate the most prominent sites
```

---

5.   en.wikipedia.org/wiki/List_of_social_networking_websites

```
def add_abbr(site):
    if site['Clusters'] == fb:
        _ = ax.annotate(site["Name"], site[columns], xytext=(1, 5),
                        textcoords="offset points", size=8,
                        color="darkslategrey")
good.apply(add_abbr, axis=1)

plt.savefig("../images/mosn.png")
```

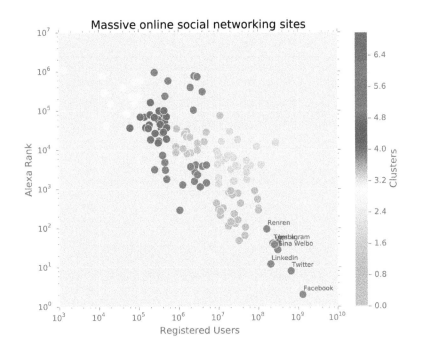

Bibliography

[BE05]   Ulrik Brandes and Thomas Erleback. *Network Analysis: Methodological Foundations*. Springer, New York, NY, 2005.

[BKL09]   Steven Bird, Ewan Klein, and Edward Loper. *Natural Language Processing with Python*. O'Reilly & Associates, Inc., Sebastopol, CA, 2009.

[For05]   Ben Forta. *MySQL Crash Course*. Sams Publishing, Indianapolis, IN, 2005.

[Gru15]   Joel Grus. *Data Science from Scratch: First Principles with Python*. O'Reilly & Associates, Inc., Sebastopol, CA, 2015.

[JWHT13] Gareth James, Daniela Witten, Trevor Hastie, and Robert Tibshirani. *An Introduction to Statistical Learning with Applications in R*. Springer, New York, NY, 2013.

[KY07]   David Knoke and Song Yang. *Social Network Analysis*. SAGE Publications, Thousand Oaks, CA, 2nd, 2007.

[Lee15]   Jeff Leek. *The Elements of Data Analytic Style*. Leanpub, Victoria, BC, Canada, 2015.

[McK12]   Wes McKinney. *Python for Data Analysis*. O'Reilly & Associates, Inc., Sebastopol, CA, 2012.

[Rus11]   Matthew A. Russell. *Mining the Social Web*. O'Reilly & Associates, Inc., Sebastopol, CA, 2011.

[ZM14]   Nina Zumel and John Mount. *Practical Data Science with R*. Manning Publications Co., Greenwich, CT, 2014.

Index

SYMBOLS

" (double quotes), xv

""" (triple double quotes), xv

$ (dollar sign), regular expressions, 21

& (and operator), 69, 78

' (single quotes), xv

''' (triple quotes), xv

() (parentheses)
    generator expression, 16
    order of operations, 70

* (asterisk)
    globbing, 26
    multiplication in numpy, 71
    regular expressions, 21
    replication in Python, 71

+ (plus sign), regular expressions, 21

- (dash)
    not operator, 69
    regular expressions, 22

. (period), regular expressions, 21

? (question mark)
    globbing, 26
    regular expressions, 21

[] (square brackets), JSON arrays, 36

[^a-d], regular expressions, 21

\ (backslash), regular expressions, 22

^ (caret), regular expressions, 21–22

{} (curly brackets), JSON objects, 36

| (or operator), 69, 78

α complexity parameter, 163

A

a, regular expressions, 21

[a-d], regular expressions, 21

ab, regular expressions, 21

accumulator, chunking, 118

accuracy of predictive experiments, 159, 165

add(), 73

add_edge(), 127, 132

add_edges_from(), 127

add_node(), 127, 132

add_nodes_from(), 127, 132

addition
    numpy, 71
    pandas, 109

adjacency lists, reading/writing from, 133

aggregating
    arrays, 76
    databases, 85
    MongoDB documents, 59
    pandas, 85, 110–112
    selections in MySQL, 53

Alexa page ranking, 171, 182

all(), 75

alphabetic characters
    checking for, 10
    regular expressions, 21

ALTER TABLE, 50

American Pie project, 146, 180

Anaconda distribution
    modules, xv
    size, 9

analysis sequence, data, 3–4

analysis types, data, 3

and operator (&), 69, 78

Andrews curves, 143

andrews_curves(), 143

annotate(), 140

any(), 75

APIs
    JSON use, 36
    resources, 173

area parameter value, 143

area plots, 143

argmax(), 107

arithmetic
    numpy arrays, 71
    pandas, 85, 109
    universal functions, 73

arrange(), 66

array(), 64

arrays
    aggregating and ordering arrays, 76
    broadcasting, 71, 76
    conditional functions, 75
    converting binary arrays to strings, 10
    copying, 64, 66
    creating, 64–66
    frames, 88
    indexing, 69
    JSON, 36
    lists as, 13, 64
    projects, 82, 178
    reading, 79

reshaping, 67
saving, 79
series, 87
slicing, 69
synthetic sine wave, 80
transposing, 66–67
treating as sets, 78
universal functions, 72–73, 76
arrow(), 140
ascending parameter, 105
aspect ratio, plotting, 137
aspect="auto" option, 137
assertions, regular expressions, 21
asterisk (*)
    globbing, 26
    multiplication in numpy, 71
    regular expressions, 21
    replication in Python, 71
asymmetric distribution, 150
asymptotes, 163
atomic data types, JSON, 36
attributes
    edges, 122, 132
    HTML, 30, 33
    network analysis, 122, 132
    nodes, 122, 132
authentication, getting data from web, 19
auto option value, 137
autocorrelation_plot(), 143
autocorrelations, 143
automating, pipeline, 6
AVG() (MySQL function), 53
axes
    descriptive statistics, 106
    plotting, 137, 140
    swapping in arrays, 68
axis, 106

B
\b, regular expressions, 21
b notation, 10
backslash (\), regular expressions, 22
backward fills, 94, 100
bar(), 139
bar parameter value, 143
bar plots, 139, 143
barh(), 139

barh parameter value, 143
BeautifulSoup, 31
    normalization example, 42
    using, 31–33
    version, xv
bell curve, see normal distribution
Bernoulli distribution, 149
best_partition(), 133
betweenness centrality, 125, 131
betweenness_centrality(), 131
bfill option value, 94, 100
big data analysis, 2
binary arrays, strings as, 10
binary confusion matrix, 158, 165
binary mode
    files, 18, 27
    network analysis, 133
    pickling, 27
binary predictive model, 158
binomial(), 152
binomial distribution, 148–149, 152
bins, discretization, 112
bit-wise operators
    order of operations, 70
    universal functions, 73
bitwise_and(), 73
bolding, finding tags, 33
Boolean attributes, graph edges and nodes, 122
Boolean operators
    indexing and slicing, 69
    order of operations, 70
    pandas, 85
Boolean values
    indexing, 69, 73, 76
    sorting by, 105
Boston, Hedonic Prices of Census Tracts, 169
bottom na_option, 106
box parameter value, 143
box plots, 139, 143
boxplot(), 139
brackets, JSON arrays and objects, 36
bridges, graphs, 123

broadcasting
    arrays, 71, 76
    frames and series, 91
broken link detector project, 44, 176

C
C, logistic (logit) regression, 163
c dot color option, 143
cache directory, 119
California population plotting project, 146
canvas, clearing plot, 138
capitalize(), 10
capturing groups, regular expressions, 21, 25
caret (^), regular expressions, 21–22
Cascading Style Sheets (CSS), 31
case
    checking for, 10
    converting, 10
    converting in normalization, 41
    ignoring in regular expressions, 21
    searching regular expressions, 24
    stop words, 41
categories, discretization, 112
causal data analysis, 3
causation, 151
CC(A), 124
centrality, 125, 131, 134, 179
centroids, 166
CHAR data type, 49
character classes, regular expressions, 21
checks, predicate functions, 10
child tags, BeautifulSoup, 32
chunking, 116, 118
chunksize, 118
cleaning data
    about, 3
    Boolean indexing, 69
    handling missing data, 98–100
    imputation, 94, 99
    replacing values, 100
    skipping data, 116
clear(), 128

clearing
  nodes and edges, 128
  plot canvas, 138
clf(), 138
clipboard, reading with pandas, 118
cliques, 124, 132
close(), 18
closeness centrality, 125, 131
closeness_centrality(), 131
cluster, 166
cluster_centers_, 166
clustering
  coefficients, 124, 130
  hierarchical, 157
  k-means, 157, 166–168
  projects, 171, 182
clustering coefficient, node, 124, 130
clustering() function, 130
cmap parameter, 137
cmudict corpus, 39
code
  project reports, 7
  reproducible, 6
  solutions to projects, 175–182
coef_, 160
coefficients
  clustering, 124, 130
  fitting linear regressions, 160, 163
collections
  counting, 17
  membership, 108
  MongoDB, 57–60
collections module, 17
collinearity, 163
color, plotting, 137, 140, 143
colorbar(), 138
colspecs, 118
columns
  aggregating data, 110
  chunking, 118
  concatenating, 103
  cross-tabulation, 114
  CSV files, 34
  data labeling, 83, 92–97
  deleting duplicates, 104
  discretization, 113
  frames, 88
  indexing, 92, 94–97, 103
  mapping, 114

merging frames and series, 101–103
  mutation, 52
  MySQL databases, 50
  name extraction, 116
  reading fixed-width data with pandas, 118
  reading tabular files with pandas, 116
  selection, 52
  stacking and pivoting, 96–97
  transposing arrays, 67
  UNIQUE constraint, 50
combine_first(), 100
comma separated values, see CSV files
command line, MySQL, 51–54
commented lines, saving and reading arrays, 79
commit(), MySQL queries, 56
communities, network
  defined, 124
  finding, 133
  partitioning, 133
  projects, 134, 156, 179
community forums, xvi
community module
  about, 121
  installing, xv, 133
  projects, 134, 179
  understanding, 124
  using, 133
  version, xv
compile(), 21
complete graphs, 122
complex network analysis, see network analysis
components, graphs, 123, 131
concat(), 103–104
concatenating, frames, 83, 103–104
conditional functions, 75
confusion matrix, 158, 165
confusion_matrix(), 165
connect(), MySQL databases, 55
connected components, graphs, 123, 131
connected_component_subgraphs(), 131
connected_components(), 131
constants, imputing, 100

continuous distribution, 148
continuous variables, converting to discrete, 112–114
Continuum Analytics, xv
contour(), 137
contour plot, 137
contourf(), 137
converting
  binary arrays and strings, 10
  case, 10, 41
  continuous variables to discrete, 112–114
  dates to numbers for Scik-it-Learn, 161
  dictionaries to series, 117
  directed graphs into undirected graphs, 130
  lists to sets, 13
  markup to plain text with BeautifulSoup, 32
  MySQL to MongoDB project, 61
  Python data structures to JSON, 36
copy(), 66
copying
  with asterisk (*), 71
  numpy arrays, 64, 66
corpora, 38–40
corpus, 38–40
correlation, 150, 153–156, 181
cos(), 73
CouchDB, 57, 60
count()
  aggregating data, 110
  MongoDB documents, 59
  pandas, 106
  strings, 12
COUNT() (MySQL function), 53
count parameter in regular expressions, 25
Counter, 17, 40, 78
counters
  using, 17
  word frequency, 28, 40, 175
counting
  aggregating data, 53, 110
  with counters, 17
  MongoDB documents, 59
  pandas, 106, 110
  substrings, 12

values, 108
word frequency, 28, 40, 175
covariance, 150, 153
CREATE, 48
cross-tabulation
    correlation example, 155
    pandas, 114
    projects, 119
crowdsourcing, 166
CSS (Cascading Style Sheets), 31
CSV files
    about, 5, 34
    chunking, 118
    HEI locator project, 82
    reading with pandas, 116
    using, 34
csv module, 34
cummax(), 107
cummin(), 107
cumprod(), 76, 107
cumsum(), 76, 107
cumulative maximum, 107
cumulative minimum, 107
cumulative product, 76, 107
cumulative sum, 76, 107
curly brackets ({}), JSON objects, 36
cut(), discretization, 112

D

\D, regular expressions, 21
\d, regular expressions, 21
D of graphs, 123
dash (-)
    not operator, 69
    regular expressions, 22
data, see also cleaning data; missing data; network data; numerical tabular data; plain text data; tabular data; test data; text data; training data
    acquisition, 5
    in data analysis sequence, 3
    extraction projects, 28, 175
    formats, 5
    raw data in project reports, 7
    sources, 5
data alignment, 110, 154

data analysis, see also frames; machine learning; network analysis; numerical tabular data; plotting; statistics
    about, 1
    big data analysis, 2
    sequence, 3–4
    types, 3
data frames, see frames
data mining, see frames; series
data model
    data analysis sequence, 4
    predictive experiments, 158
data science
    analysis sequence, 3
    overview, 1–8
    report structure, 7
    resources, xvi, 173
Data Science from Scratch, 174
Data Science Stack Exchange forum, xvi
data series, see series
data structures
    choosing, 13
    converting to JSON, 36
    pandas, 85–91
    types, 13
data types
    JSON, 36
    MySQL, 49
    numpy arrays, 64, 66
    pandas, 108
    type narrowing, 66
data visualization, see also graphs; plotting; visualization
    about, 1
    Gephi, 126, 131, 133–134
    projects, 146, 180
Data.gov, 34
database cursor, 55
database driver module, 55
database schemas, 49
databases, 47–61, see also MySQL
    about, 1, 47
    aggregating, 85
    as data source, 5
    connecting to, 55
    CouchDB, 57, 60
    creating, 48

creating tables, 48
deleting records, 50, 52
dropping tables, 49
indexing and performance, 50
inserting records, 50–51
MongoDB, xv, 47, 57–61
projects, 61, 176
resources, 174
schemas, 49
DataFrame(), 92, 95
DATE data type, 49
date plots, 139
dates
    converting to numbers for SciKit-Learn, 161
    databases, 49, 51
    datetime parsing, 116
DATETIME data type, 49
decision forests, random, 169, 171
decision trees, 169
decode(), 10
decoding functions, 10
definition(), synsets, 39
degree, graph nodes, 122, 130
degree centrality, 125, 131
degree() function, 130
degree_centrality(), 131
DELETE FROM, 52
delete_many(), 60
delete_one(), 60
deleting
    duplicates in pandas, 104
    edges, 128
    indexes and deleting times, 50
    missing data, 98
    MongoDB documents, 60
    new lines, 10
    nodes, 127–128
    records, 50, 52
    rows, 93
    tables, 49–50
    tags, 32
    whitespaces, 10–11, 34
delim, 11
delimiter, 116
delimiters
    CSV files, 34
    reading tabular files with pandas, 116

saving and reading arrays, 79
string, 11
density, graphs, 122
density plots, 143
describing, data in pandas, 105–108
descriptive data analysis, 3
deserializing
    JSON, 36
    pickle module, 27
diameter, graphs, 123
dictionaries
    aggregating data by mapping, 111
    centralities, 131
    cmudict corpus, 39
    community partitioning, 133
    converting to series, 117
    creating, 13
    defined, 13
    edge, 129, 132
    frames, 88
    graphs, 132
    JSON objects, 36
    MongoDB documents as, 58
    node, 132
    series, 87
diff(), 107
differences
    descriptive statistics, 107
    partial, 82, 178
    pseudo-differentiation, 107
digital signal processing, 2
digits
    checking for, 10
    regular expressions, 21
digraphs, see directed graphs
directed graphs, 122–123, 130, 132
dirty data, defined, 3, see also cleaning data
discrete distribution, 148
discretization, 112–114
distance, measuring between graph nodes, 123
distributions, probability, 148–150, 152
division, pandas, 109
document stores
    CouchDB, 57, 60
    MongoDB, xv, 47, 57–61

documentation, series values and index names, 87
dollar sign ($), regular expressions, 21
dot sizes, plotting, 143
DOUBLE data type, 49
double quotes ("), xv
download(), nltk corpora, 40
downloading
    from Internet, 19
    nltk corpora, 40
DROP command, 49
drop() method, 93
drop_duplicates(), 104
dropna(), 98
dropping
    duplicates in pandas, 104
    missing data, 98
    rows, 93
    tables, 49
dtype parameter, 64, 66
dummy variables, 113
dump(), 37
dumps(), 37
duplicated(), 104
duplicates
    deleting in pandas, 104
    nested list comprehension, 15
    removing with sets, 13

E
eXtensible Markup Language, see XML
eXtensible Stylesheet Language Transformation (XSLT), 31
edge attribute, 129
edge lists, reading/writing from, 133
edges
    attributes, 122, 132
    bridges, 123
    clearing, 128
    dictionaries, 129, 132
    graph walks, 123
    modifying graphs, 127
    understanding graphs, 122
    weight, 122–123
edges() function, 129, 132
Eigenvector centrality, 125, 131
eigenvector_centrality(), 131

The Elements of Data Analytic Style, 173
embellishments, plotting, 140–143
emoticons, 41
empty(), 65
encode(), 10
end(), pattern matching, 24
English stop words, 38
ensemble, 169
ensembles, 169
entities
    aggregation, 112
    extraction, 38, 43
enumerate(), 13
Epinions.com, 134, 179
equal(), 73
errorbar(), 139
escaping
    backslash (\) character, 22
    delimiter characters in CSV files, 34
    regular expressions, 21
exceptions
    MySQL warnings, 51
    opening URLs, 19
execute(), MySQL databases, 55
exp(), 73
exploratory data analysis, 3
eye(), 65

F
Facebook, 36
false negative (FN), 158
false positive (FP), 158
fetchall(), MySQL databases, 55
ffill option value, 94, 100
file indexer project, 61, 176
fileids(), creating copora, 40
files, see also reading; writing
    as data source, 5
    binary mode, 18, 27
    creating copora, 40
    defined, 18
    fragments and markup tags, 32
    globbing file names, 26
    opening, 18
    pandas input/output, 116–118

projects, 28, 176
working with, 18
filled contour plot, 137
fillna(), 100
fills, 94, 100
filtering, selections in MySQL, 53
financial time series, 173
find()
    BeautifulSoup, 32
    MongoDB, 58
    strings, 11
find_all(), BeautifulSoup, 32
find_cliques(), 132
find_one(), MongoDB, 58
findall(), substrings with regular expressions, 24–25
finding
    cliques, 132
    communities, 133
    fragments, 11, 24
    glob module, 23, 26
    MongoDB documents, 58
    selecting records, 52
    strings, 11
    strings with regular expressions, 24–25
    substrings with regular expressions, 24–25
    tags with BeautifulSoup, 32
first(), aggregating data, 110
fit()
    k-means clustering, 166
    linear regressions, 160
    random decision forests, 169
fit_predict(), 166
fitting, linear regressions, 160–165
fixed-width data, reading with pandas, 118
flattening multiindexes, 96–97
FLOAT data type, 49
floating-point numbers
    FLOAT data type, 49
    IEEE 754 standard, 74, 99
    synthetic sine wave, 80
    universal functions, 73
floor(), 73
FN (false negative), 158
fonts, plotting, 140–141
forward fills, 94, 100

forward pointers, 64
FP (false positive), 158
fragments
    file fragments and markup tags, 32
    finding, 11, 24
    joining, 11
frames
    about, 83
    aggregating, 110–112
    binomial distribution of random numbers, 152
    broadcasting, 91
    centralities, 131
    combining, 100–104
    concatenating, 83, 103–104
    creating, 88
    cross-tabulation, 114
    defined, 85, 88
    deleting duplicates, 104
    descriptive statistics, 107
    discretization, 112–114
    hierarchical indexing, 94–97, 103
    indexing, 88, 92–97
    merging, 83, 100–103
    missing data, 98–100
    ordering, 105–108
    pivoting, 97
    plotting, 143–145
    projects, 119, 178
    ranking, 106
    reading tabular files with pandas, 117
    reindexing, 93
    sorting, 105
    stacking, 96
    statistical measures, 153
    transforming data, 109–115
    using, 88–91
from_tuples(), 95
functions, see conditional functions; predicate functions; universal functions

G

G(A), 124
Gaussian distribution, see normal distribution
Gaussian noise, 80
GCC (giant connected component), 123
GDP vs. alcohol consumption project, 119
generators, list, 14, 16, 131

Gephi, 126, 131, 133–134
get(), BeautifulSoup, 33
get_dummies(), 113
get_text(), 32
ggplot(), 135–138
giant connected component (GCC), 123
glob module, 23, 26, 40
globbing, 23, 26, 40
GML, 133
gnuplot, 135
Graph(), 127
graph density, 122
graph walks, 123
graphs
    building with networkx, 127
    centrality, 125, 131
    complete, 122
    density, 122
    dictionaries, 132
    directed, 122–123, 130, 132
    elements, 122
    Gephi, 126, 131, 133–134
    modifying, 127
    pie charts, 139, 143, 146, 180
    simple, 122
    structure, 123
    subgraphs, 131
    types, 122
    understanding, 122–125
    undirected, 122, 130
    walks, 123
    weighted, 122–123
greater(), 73
grid(), 138
grids, toggling, 138
group(), pattern matching, 24
GROUP BY, 53
groupby(), 110–112
grouping
    frames, 110–112
    k-means clustering, 166–168
    MongoDB documents, 59
    order of operations, 22
    regular expressions, 21, 24–25
    selections in MySQL, 53
gutenberg corpus, 38
Gutenberg Project, 38
.gz extension, 79

H

h5py, 63
has_attr(), 33
HAVING, 53
HDF5 binary data format, 63
head(), 88, 90
header, 116
headers, reading tabular files
    with pandas, 116
Hedonic Prices of Census
    Tracts in the Boston Area,
    169
HEI locator project, 82
Hello, World! project, 8, 175
hexagonal bin plots, 143
hexbin parameter value, 143
hierarchical clustering, 157
hierarchical indexing, 94–97,
    103
hist(), 139
hist parameter value, 143
histograms, 139, 143
homophones, 39
hops, 123
how parameter, 103
HTML
    as data format, 5
    attributes, 30, 33
    compared to XML, 31
    hyperlink tags, 32
    parsing with BeautifulSoup,
        31
    processing files, 30–33
    tags, 30–31
html.parser, 31
html5lib, xv, 31
hyperlinks, tags, 32
hypernyms, 39
HyperText Markup Language,
    see HTML
hyponyms, 39
hypot(), 73

I

I flag, regular expressions, 21
[i:j] slicing operation, 69
[i] indexing operation, 69
_id key, MongoDB documents,
    58
identity matrix, 65
idxmax(), 107

IEEE 754 floating-point stan-
    dard, 74, 99
IGNORE, 51
ignoring
    case, 21
    UNIQUE constraint, 51
image formats, plots, 138
imputation, 94, 99
imshow(), 137
in, 93
in1d(), 78
in_degree_centrality(), 131
incremental plotting, defined,
    135, see also plotting
indegree, 122, 130
indegree() function, 130
index attribute, series, 86
index parameter, 92
index.values attribute, series, 86
index_col, 116
indexing
    arithmetic operations,
        110
    arrays, 69
    Boolean, 69, 73, 76
    estimating correlation,
        154
    frames, 88, 92–97
    hierarchical, 94–97, 103
    latent semantic, 43
    merging indexes, 102
    MySQL databases, 50
    pandas, 85–86, 88, 92–97,
        116
    performance, 50
    projects, 28, 61, 176
    reading tabular files with
        pandas, 116
    reindexing, 93
    series, 86, 92–97
    smart, 70, 75, 93
    sorting, 105
    stacking and pivoting,
        96–97
inf, 74
inferential data analysis, 3
infinity, positive, 73–74
inner joins
    indexes, 103
    MySQL, 54
inplace=True parameter, 92, 105
input/output
    network analysis, 133
    pandas, 116–118

INSERT INTO, 51
insert_many(), MongoDB, 58
insert_one(), MongoDB, 58
inserted_id, 58
inserted_ids, 58
inserting
    indexes and inserting
        times, 50
    MongoDB documents, 58
    records, 50–51
    tables, 50
InsertManyResult, 58
InsertOneResult, 58
installing
    community module, xv, 133
    nltk, 40
INT data type, 49
intercept_, 160
intercepts, fitting linear regres-
    sions, 160
Internet
    as data source, 5
    downloading from, 19
intersect1d(), 78
intersection, 78
An Introduction to Statistical
    Learning with Applications
    in R, 156, 173
inverse regularization, 163
isalpha(), 10
isdigit(), 10
isfinite(), 73
isin(), 108
isinf(), 73
islower(), 10
isnan(), 73
isnull(), 99
isolates(), 132
isspace(), 10
isupper(), 10
italics, finding tags, 33
ix attribute, 93

J

Jaccard similarity index, 44
JavaScript Object Notation,
    see JSON
join()
    indexes, 102
    strings, 11
joining, see also merging
    fragments, 11

indexes, 102
strings, 11
tables, 54
JSON
  about, 36
  as data format, 5
  converting Python data
    structures to, 36
  data types, 36
  deserializing, 36
  reading JSON files, 36
  reading with pandas, 118
  serializing, 36
  Wikipedia project, 44
json module, xv, 36

K

k clusters, 166
k, positive, 65
k-means clustering, 157,
  166–168
kde parameter value, 143
keep, 104
keep_na_option, 106
keys
  chunking, 118
  concatenating frames,
    103
  creating dictionaries, 14
  deleting records, 52
  dictionary data structure,
    13
  frames, 88
  JSON objects, 36
  MongoDB documents as,
    58
  MySQL databases, 49
  series, 87
keys parameter, 103
kind parameter, plots, 143
KMeans() function, 167
KMeans object, 166
kseq, 14

L

"_l" suffix, 102
labels
  discretization, 112
  k-means clustering, 166
  nodes, 127
  pandas, 83, 92–97
  plotting, 138
labels parameter, 112
labels_, 166
lag plots, 143

lag_plot(), 143
Lancaster stemmer, 41
languages, see natural language processing (NLP)
last(), aggregating data, 110
last modification timestamp,
  49
latent semantic indexing, 43
layered plotting, 135
LDA (linear discriminant
  analysis), 159
left joins
  indexes, 103
  MySQL, 54
"left" how parameter, 103
left_index=True, 102
left_shift(), 73
legend(), 140
legends, plotting, 140, 143
lemmatization, 42
lemmatize(), 42
len()
  network analysis, 129
  series, 86
less(), 73
line plots, 139, 143
linear discriminant analysis
  (LDA), 159
linear regression, 160–165
linear search time and data
  structures, 13
linear_model module, 160, 163
LinearRegression(), 160
links
  broken link detector
    project, 44, 176
  hyperlink tags, 32
links variable in BeautifulSoup, 33
list(), 14, 131
list comprehension, 15, 33
lists
  as arrays, 13, 64
  comprehension, 15, 33
  connected components,
    131
  converting to sets, 13
  defined, 13
  generators, 14, 16, 131
  joining strings, 11
  neighbors, 129
  nodes, 129
  replacing values, 100

load()
  arrays, 79
  JSON files, 37
  pickling files, 27
loads(), JSON files, 37
loadtxt(), 79
local clustering coefficient,
  node, 124, 130
log(), 73, 109
log plots, 139
log-log plots, 139
log10(), 109
logical universal functions, 73
logical_not(), 73
logistic (logit) regression, 163
logistic function, 163
LogisticRegression(), 163
loglog(), 139
long tail distributions, 149
loops, graphs, 122–123
Louvain method, 133
lower(), 10
lowercase
  converting in normaliza-
    tion, 41
  converting strings, 10
  stop words, 41
lstrip(), 10
lsuffix parameter, 103
lxml.parser, 31
lynx trapping project, 119,
  178

M

M flag, regular expressions,
  21
machine learning, 157–171
  about, 2, 157
  dummy variables, 113
  k-means clustering, 157,
    166–168
  linear regression, 160–
    165
  predictive experiment
    setup, 158
  projects, 171, 182
  random decision forests,
    169, 171
  resources, 174
many-to-many merging, 101
map(), 114
mapping, 111, 114

markup
    fragments and, 32
    parser, 31
massive online social network-
    ing (MOSN) project, 171,
    182
master plots, 137
match(), strings with regular
    expressions, 24
matching, *see* pattern match-
    ing
mathematics
    cumulative products, 76,
        107
    cumulative sums, 76,
        107
    numpy, 71, 73
    pandas, 85, 109
    universal functions, 73
matplotlib
    basic plotting, 136–138
    ggplot style, 135
    synthetic sine wave, 81
    version, xv
matrices
    identity, 65
    multiplication, 65
    rounding, 72
    scatter, 143
    transposing arrays, 68
max()
    aggregating data, 110
    numpy, 76
    pandas, 106
MAX() (MySQL function), 53
maximal clique, 124, 132
maximum
    cumulative, 107
    universal functions, 73
maximum clique, 124
maxsplit, 23
McKinney, Wes, 173
mean()
    aggregating data, 110
    defined, 150
    numpy, 76
    pandas, 106
    project, 156, 181
    statistics module, 153
mechanistic data analysis, 3
median(), 106, 110
MediaWiki project, 44
membership, 108
merge(), 101–104

merging
    frames, 83, 100–103
    indexes, 102
    series, 100–103
method parameter, 94
metrics, 165
min()
    aggregating data, 110
    numpy, 76
    pandas, 106
MIN() (MySQL function), 53
minimum
    cumulative, 107
    universal functions, 73
Mining the Social Web, 173
missing data
    about, 3
    deleting, 98
    imputation, 94, 99
    pandas, 85, 98–100, 116
MIT, 134
model score, 160
modularity, 124, 133
modularity() function, 133
modules, versions table, xv
MongoClient, 57
MongoDB
    about, xv, 47
    compared to CouchDB,
        60
    using, 57–61
monolithic plotting, 135
most_common(), 17
multigraphs, 122
multiindexes, 94–97, 103
multiline mode, regular ex-
    pressions, 21
multiplication
    cumulative products, 76,
        107
    matrices, 65
    numpy, 71
    pandas, 109
    universal functions, 73
multiply(), 73
music genre classifier project,
    44
mutation, 52
MySQL
    about, xv, 47
    command line, 51–54
    connecting to databases,
        55
    data types, 49

grouping and aggregating
    results, 53
inserting records, 51–52
joining tables, 54
mutation, 52
order of operations, 53
ordering, 53
projects, 61, 176
pymysql module, xv, 55
resources, 174
selection, 52
setup, 48–50
mysql client, 48–50
MySQL Crash Course, 174

N
\n, regular expressions, 21
n_clusters, 167
na_option, 106
na_position, 105
na_values, 116
naive Bayes classification,
    157, 159
names
    extracting in pandas, 116
    frames, 88
    globbing file, 26
    names corpus, 38
    reading tabular files with
        pandas, 116
    series values and index,
        87
    sorting by in pandas, 105
names corpus, 38
names parameter, 116
nan
    about, 74, 98
    counting values, 108
    descriptive statistics, 106
    imputation, 99
    merging, 101
    ranking data, 106
National Climatic Data Cen-
    ter, 119
National Institute on Alcohol
    Abuse and Alcoholism (NI-
    AAA)
    data set, 89
    k-means clustering exam-
        ple, 167
    plotting examples, 136,
        140, 143
    series and frames exam-
        ple, 89, 94
    statistics example, 153
natural joins, MySQL, 54

natural language processing
(NLP), 1, 38–43, 173
*Natural Language Processing
with Pythons*, 173
Natural Language Toolkit,
see nltk
ndim, 65
negative(), 73
negative skewness, 150
negative, false, 158
negative, true, 158
neighborhoods, 124
neighbors, lists, 129
neighbors() function, 129
nested list comprehension, 15
network analysis, 121–134
about, 1
building a network, 127
centrality, 125, 131,
134, 179
graphs, understanding,
122–125
input/output, 133
projects, 134, 156, 179
Really Large Networks,
130
resources, 174
sequence, 126
using networkx, 127–133
*Network Analysis: Methodolog-
ical Foundations*, 174
network data, defined, 121
NetworKit, 130
networkx
about, 121, 126
input/output, 133
projects, 134
using, 127–133
version, xv
neural networks, 157, 159
new lines
read/write functions, 18
removing, 10
newaxis object, 160
next tags, BeautifulSoup, 32
NIAAA, *see* National Institute
on Alcohol Abuse and Alcoholism, National Institute
on Alcohol Abuse and Alcoholism (NIAAA)
NLP, *see* natural language
processing (NLP)
nltk, 38–43
installing, 40

projects, 61, 176
using, 38–43
version, xv
node attribute, 129
nodes
attributes, 122, 132
centrality, 125, 131,
134, 179
clearing, 128
cliques, 124, 132
community, 124, 133–
134, 179
degree, 122, 130
dictionaries, 132
lists, 129
local clustering coeffi-
cient, 124, 130
measuring distance, 123
modifying graphs, 127
neighborhoods, 124
neighbors, 129
projects, 134, 156
stars, 124
supernodes, 126
understanding graphs,
122
nodes() function, 129
noise
random, 71
synthetic sine wave, 80
non-capturing groups, regular
expressions, 25
nonzero(), 75
normal(), 152
normal distribution, 148–149
normalization
case conversion, 10, 41
performance, 56
using, 41–43
NoSQL, CouchDB, 57, 60, *see
also* MongoDB
NOT NULL keyword, 49
not operator (-), 69
not-a-number
about, 74, 98
counting values, 108
descriptive statistics, 106
imputation, 99
merging, 101
ranking data, 106
notes, plotting, 140
notnull(), 99
NOW(), 51
.npy extension, 79

numeric data analysis, defined, 1, *see also* numerical
tabular data
Numeric Python, *see* numpy
numerical tabular data, 63–
82
about, 63
aggregating and ordering
arrays, 76
arrays, creating, 64–66
broadcasting, 71, 76
conditional functions, 75
indexing, 69
projects, 82, 178
reshaping, 67
saving and reading ar-
rays, 79
slicing, 69
synthetic sine wave, 80
transposing, 66–67
treating arrays as sets,
78
universal functions, 72–
73, 76, 109
numpy, 63–82
about, 63, 82, 178
aggregating and ordering
arrays, 76
arrays, creating, 64–66
broadcasting, 71, 76
conditional functions, 75
indexing, 69
.npy extension, 79
performance, 64
projects, 82, 178
random numbers, 152
reshaping, 67
resources, 173
saving and reading ar-
rays, 79
slicing, 69
slicing in linear regres-
sions, 160
statistics with random
module, 152
synthetic sine wave, 80
transposing, 66–67
treating arrays as sets,
78
universal functions, 72–
73, 76, 109
version, xv
numpy.newaxis object, 160
numpy.random module, 152
nutrients project, 156

O

objects
    chunking, 118
    JSON, 36–37
observations, 34
Occam's razor principle, 29
OLS (ordinary least square
    regression), 160, 171
on parameter, 103
one-to-many merging, 101
one-to-one merging, 101
ones(), 65
open(), 18, 27
or operator (|), 69, 78
ORDER BY, 53
order of operations
    bit-wise operators, 70
    Boolean operators, 70
    regular expressions, 22
    selections in MySQL, 53
ordering
    arrays, 76
    data in pandas, 102, 105–
      108
    frames, 105–108
    merging indexes, 102
    series, 105–108
ordinary least square (OLS)
    regression, 160, 171
orientation, arrays, 67
out_degree_centrality(), 131
outdegree, 122, 130
outdegree() function, 130
outer joins
    indexes, 103
    MySQL, 54
output
    network analysis, 133
    pandas, 116–118

P

p-value, 151, 154, 162
Pajek, 133
pandas, 83–119
    about, 83
    aggregation, 110–112
    combining data, 101–104
    cross-tabulation, 114
    data structures, 85–91
    deleting duplicates, 104
    discretization, 112–114
    file input/output, 116–
      118

    hierarchical indexing, 94–
      97, 103
    indexing, 85–86, 88, 92–
      97, 116
    mapping, 111, 114
    merging in, 101–103
    missing data, 85, 98–
      100, 116
    ordering and describing
      data, 102, 105–108
    plotting, 85, 143–145
    projects, 119, 178
    reading other formats,
      118
    reading tabular files, 116
    reindexing, 93
    reshaping data, 92–97
    resources, 173
    statistics, 106, 152–153
    transforming data, 109–
      115
    treating series as sets,
      108
    version, xv
pandas.tools.plotting module, 143
parent tags, BeautifulSoup, 32
parentheses (())
    generator expression, 16
    order of operations, 70
Pareto distribution, 149
parse, 19, 23
parsing
    datetime, 116
    HTML and XML with
      BeautifulSoup, 31
    URLs, 19, 23
part-of-speech (POS) tagging,
    42
partial differences, 82, 178
partial sums, 82, 178
partitioning, communities,
    133
path_similarity(), 39
paths, graphs, 123
pattern matching
    globbing, 23, 26
    regular expressions, 21–
      25
PCA (principal component
    analysis), 43, 157
PDF (probability density
    function), 148–149
Pearson correlation coeffi-
    cient, 150, 154
pearsonr(), 154

performance
    indexing, 50
    network analysis, 130
    normalization, 56
    numpy, 64
    set operations, 78
period (.), regular expressions,
    21
Perl, regular expressions, 23
phone number extractor, 28
pickle module, 18, 27, 37
pickling data, 27, 37
pie(), 139
pie charts, 139, 143, 146,
    180
pie parameter value, 143
pipeline
    automation, 6
    data acquisition, 5
pivot(), 97
pivoting multiindexes, 96–97
plain text data
    converting markup to, 32
    format, 5
PlaintextCorpusReader, 40
plot(), 135, 139, 143
plot_dates(), 139
plotting, 135–146
    about, 135
    approaches, 135
    bar plots, 139, 143
    basic plotting, 136–138
    box plots, 139, 143
    contour plots, 137
    date plots, 139
    density plots, 143
    embellishments, 140–143
    ggplot(), 135
    gnuplot, 135
    hexagonal bin plots, 143
    histograms, 139, 143
    lag plots, 143
    line plots, 139, 143
    log plots, 139
    with pandas, 85, 143–145
    plot types, 139
    polar plots, 139
    projects, 146, 180
    pyplot, 84, 135–146
    scatter plots, 139, 143
    step plots, 139
    subplots, 137
    Unicode, 141
    xkcd plots, 141
    xyplot(), 135

plus sign (+), regular expressions, 21
PMF (probability mass function), 148
polar(), 139
polar plots, 139
population plotting project, 146
Porter stemmer, 41
(POS) part-of-speech tagging, 42
pos_tag(), 42
positive infinity, 73–74
positive k, 65
positive, false, 158
positive, true, 158
postal addresses extractor, 28
power law distribution, 149
Practical Data Science with R, 173
precision of predictive experiments, 159
predicate functions, 10
predict()
    k-means clustering, 166
    linear regressions, 160
    logistic (logit) regression, 163
    random decision forests, 169
predictive data analysis
    binomial distribution of random numbers, 152
    defined, 3
    modeling, 4
    setup, 158
preprocessing, 166
prettify(), 32
pretty printing, 32
previous tags, BeautifulSoup, 32
principal component analysis (PCA), 43, 157
probability
    about, 147
    distributions, 148–150, 152
    projects, 156, 181
probability density function (PDF), 148–149
probability mass function (PMF), 148
prod(), aggregating data, 110

products
    aggregating data, 110
    cumulative, 76, 107
project reports, structure, 7
projects
    American Pie, 146, 180
    arrays, 82, 178
    broken link detector, 44, 176
    California population plotting, 146
    data extraction, 28, 44, 175
    databases, 61, 176
    difficulty rankings, xvi
    file indexer, 61, 176
    GDP vs. alcohol consumption, 119
    HEI locator project, 82
    Hello, World!, 8, 175
    indexing, 28, 61, 176
    lynx trapping, 119, 178
    machine learning, 171, 182
    massive online social networking, 171, 182
    MediaWiki, 44
    MongoDB, 61
    music genre classifier, 44
    network analysis, 134, 156, 179
    numpy, 82, 178
    nutrients analysis, 156
    pandas, 119, 178
    phone number extractor, 28
    plotting, 146, 180
    postal addresses extractor, 28
    probability, 156, 181
    regular expressions, 28, 175
    S&P, 156, 171, 181
    Shakespeare, 134
    solutions, 175–182
    state similarity calculator, 82
    statistics, 156, 181
    subway predictor, 171
    text data, 44
    weather vs. alcohol consumption project, 119
    word frequency counter, 28, 40, 175
pronunciation dictionary corpus, 39
pseudo random seed, 152
pseudo-differentiation, 107

pseudo-integration, 107
Punch, John, 29
punctuation, 41
pymongo, xv, 57–61
pymysql, xv, 55
pyplot
    as incremental plotting, 135
    basic plotting, 136–138
    embellishments, 140–142
    pandas integration, 84, 143–145
    plot types, 139
    resources, 139
    using, 135–146
Python
    complexity, xiii, 9
    core overview, 9–28
    module versions table, xv
    resources, 173
    versions, xv
Python for Data Analysis, 173

Q
qcuts(), 113
quality assurance, predictive experiments, 158
quantifiers, regular expressions, 21
quantities, discretization, 113
queries, MySQL, 50, 55
question mark (?)
    globbing, 26
    regular expressions, 21
quotes, xv, 34

R
R^2, 160
\r, regular expressions, 21
R language, resources, 156, 173, *see also* pandas, plotting
"_r" suffix, 102
rand(), 152
randint(), 152
randn(), 152
random decision forests, 169, 171
random module, 152
random noise, 71
random numbers
    generating, 152
    probability distributions, 148–149

random seed, 152
RandomForestRegressor(), 169
range(), 14, 66
rank(), 106
ranking, frames and series, 106
raw(), creating copora, 40
re module, 21–25
re.I flag, 21
re.M flag, 21
read(), 18–19
read(n), 18
read_adjlist(), 133
read_clipboard(), 118
read_csv(), 116, 118
read_edgelist(), 133
read_fwf(), 118
read_gml(), 133
read_graphml(), 133
read_json(), 118
read_pajek(), 133
read_table(), 117–118
reading
    arrays, 79
    CSV files, 34, 116, 118
    data with pandas, 85, 116
    files, 18–19, 27
    fixed-width data, 118
    JSON files, 36
    JSON files with pandas, 118
    network analysis, 133
    with pandas, 118
    tabular data, 116
readline(), 18–19
readlines(), 18–19
README file, 7
Really Large Networks, 130
recall of predictive experiments, 159
records
    deleting, 50, 52
    inserting, 50–51
recursive web crawling, 33
regexp_tokenize(), 41
regression
    linear, 160–165
    logistic (logit), 163
    ordinary least square, 160, 171
    random decision forests, 169, 171
    ridge, 163

regular expressions
    defined, 21
    examples, 23
    finding substrings, 24–25
    glob module, 23, 26
    matching strings, 24
    operators, list of, 21
    order of operations, 22
    Perl, 23
    projects, 28, 175
    reading tabular files with pandas, 116
    removing whitespaces, 11
    replacing strings, 25
    searching strings, 24–25
    splitting strings, 23
    tokenization, 41
    using, 21–25
regularization, 163
regularization, inverse, 163
reindexing, 93
relational databases, 48, 56, see also databases; MySQL
relational universal functions, 73
repl, 25
replace(), 100
replacing
    strings with regular expressions, 25
    values, 100
replication with asterisk (*), 71
reports, structure, 7
reproducible code, 6
request module, 19
reset_index(), 92
reshape(), 67, 92
reshaping
    numpy, 67
    pandas, 92–97
residuals, 160
resources
    APIs, 173
    for this book, xvi
    data science, xvi, 173
    databases, 174
    further reading, 173
    Gephi, 133
    machine learning, 174
    MySQL, 174
    natural language processing (NLP), 173
    network analysis, 174
    numpy, 173

pandas, 173
pyplot, 139
Python, 173
statistics, 156, 174
Ridge(), 163
ridge regression, 163
right joins
    indexes, 103
    MySQL, 54
"right" how parameter, 103
right_index=True, 102
round(), 72
rounding, matrices, 72
rows
    aggregating data, 110
    concatenating, 103
    cross-tabulation, 114
    CSV files, 34
    data labeling, 83, 92–97
    deleting duplicates, 104
    dropping, 93
    indexing, 93
    merging frames and series, 101–103
    skipping when reading tabular files with pandas, 116
    transposing arrays, 67
rstrip(), 10
rsuffix parameter, 103

S
\S, regular expressions, 21
\s, regular expressions, 21
s dot size option, 143
S&P
    linear regression example, 161
    OLS (ordinary least square regression) project, 171
    Twenty-First Century project, 156, 181
s-curve, logistic (logit) regression, 163
sampling
    about, 151
    defined, 126
    k-means clustering, 166–168
    network analysis, 126
save(), 79
savefig(), 138
savetxt(), 79

saving
    arrays, 79
    plots, 138
scale(), 166
scaling
    changing axes, 140
    variables for k-means
        clustering, 166
scatter(), 139
scatter matrices, 143
scatter parameter value, 143
scatter plots, 139, 143
scatter_matrix(), 143
schemas, database, 49
scientific discovery sequence,
    3
SciKit-Learn, xv, 157–171
scipy, xv, 152, 154
scipy.stats module, 152, 154
score(), 160
search(), 24–25
searching, *see* finding
Secure Sockets Layer (SSL),
    19
seed(), 152
segmentation, 43
SELECT, 52
selection, 52
semantic indexing, latent, 43
semantic similarity, 39, 44
semilogx(), 139
semilogy(), 139
sensitivity of predictive exper-
    iments, 159
sent(), 41
sentence tokenization, 38, 41
sentences
    creating copora, 40
    tokenization, 38, 41
sentiment analysis, 38, 41,
    43
sents(), creating copora, 40
sep, 116
separators
    CSV files, 34
    reading tabular files with
        pandas, 116
seq, 13
sequence of data analysis, 3
sequence of network analysis,
    126

serializing
    JSON, 36
    pickle module, 27
series
    about, 83
    aggregating, 110–112
    broadcasting, 91
    centralities, 131
    combining, 100–104
    converting from dictionar-
        ies, 117
    creating, 85
    defined, 85
    deleting duplicates, 104
    descriptive statistics, 107
    dictionaries, 87
    discretization, 112–114
    hierarchical indexing, 94–
        97, 103
    indexing, 86, 92–97
    merging, 100–103
    missing data, 98–100
    ordering, 105–108
    plotting, 143–145
    projects, 119, 178
    ranking, 106
    reindexing, 93
    sorting, 105
    statistical measures, 153
    transforming data, 109–
        115
    treating as sets, 108
    using, 85–88
SET, 52
set_index(), 92
sets
    binomial distribution of
        random numbers, 152
    converting lists to, 13
    defined, 13
    performance and set oper-
        ations, 78
    treating arrays as, 78
    treating series as, 108
Shakespeare works project,
    134
Shakespeare, William, 134
shape option, generating ran-
    dom numbers, 152
shape variable, arrays, 65
shapes
    arrays, 65
    generating random num-
        bers, 152
show(), plots, 138
SHOW WARNINGS, 51

sigmoid, logistic (logit) regres-
    sion, 163
similarity, 39, 44, 82
simple graphs, 122
sin(), 73
sine wave, generating, 80
single quotes ('), xv
singular value decomposition
    (SVD), 43
size, generating random num-
    bers, 152
skewness, 150, 156, 181
skipna, 106
skipping
    descriptive statistics, 106
    rows in reading tabular
        files with pandas, 116
    saving and reading ar-
        rays, 79
    unclean data, 116
skiprows, 116
sklearn.cluster, 166
sklearn.ensemble, 169
sklearn.linear_model module,
    160, 163
sklearn.metrics, 165
sklearn.preprocessing, 166
slicing
    arrays, 69
    linear regressions, 160
    smart, 70
SMALLINT data type, 49
smart indexing, 70, 75, 93
smart slicing, 70
snowballing, 124
social networks
    massive online social
        networking project,
        171, 182
    resources, 173
solutions to projects, 175–182
sort()
    arrays, 77
    MongoDB documents, 59
sort_index(), 105
sort_values(), 105
sorting
    arrays, 76
    frames, 105
    indexes, 105
    merging indexes, 102
    MongoDB documents, 59

selection in MySQL, 53
series, 105
soup, *see* BeautifulSoup
spaces, checking for, 10
specificity of predictive experiments, 159
split(), 11, 23
splitting
    aggregating data, 110
    data for predictive experiments, 158
    for plotting, 136
    strings, 11, 23
SQL, *see* MySQL
sqrt(), 73
square brackets ([]), JSON arrays, 36
squared residuals (SSR), 160
SSL (Secure Sockets Layer), 19
SSR (squared residuals), 160
stack(), 96
stacking multiindexes, 96–97
standard deviation
    aggregating data, 110
    defined, 150
    numpy, 76
    pandas, 106
    project, 156, 181
    statistics module, 153
Stanford Large Network Dataset Collection, 134, 179
stars, graphs, 124
start(), pattern matching, 24
start variable, arrange(), 66
state similarity calculator project, 82
statistical inference, 151
statistics, 147–156
    CSV file example, 35
    defined, 147
    measures review, 150
    modules, 152–155
    pandas, 106, 152–153
    projects, 156, 181
    resources, 156, 174
Statistics Canada, 104
statistics module
    CSV file example, 35
    using, 152–153
std()
    aggregating data, 110

numpy, 76
pandas, 106
stdev(), statistics module, 153
stem(), 41
stemming
    normalization, 41
    projects, 44, 134
step() function, plots, 139
step plots, 139
step variable, arrange(), 66
stop variable, arrange(), 66
stop words, 38, 41
stopwords corpus, 38, 41
storing
    data with CSV files, 34
    JSON files, 36
    pickled files, 27
str, 10–12
straight joins, MySQL, 54
strings
    binary arrays, 10
    case conversion, 10
    decoding, 10
    defined, 10
    defining raw strings in regular expressions, 22
    finding, 11
    functions, 10–12
    globbing, 26
    graph edge and node attributes, 122
    joining, 11
    JSON, 36
    predicate functions, 10
    quote notation, xv
    regular expressions, 21–25
    removing whitespaces and tabs, 10–11
    splitting, 11, 23
strip(), 10
stripped_strings variable, 32
stripping, *see also* deleting
    tags with BeautifulSoup, 32
    whitespaces, 10, 34
strongly_connected_components(), 131
structured data
    format, 5
    processing HTML/XML files, 30–33
Structured Query Language, *see* MySQL

styling
    CSS, 31
    plotting, 137, 140–141, 143
sub(), regular expressions, 25
subgraph(), 131
subgraphs, 131
sublinear O(log(N)) search time and data structures, 13
subplot() function, 137
subplots, 137
substrings
    finding, 24–25
    splitting, 11, 23
subtraction, pandas, 109
subway predictor project, 171
suffixes, merging indexes, 102–103
suffixes parameter, 102
sum()
    aggregating data, 110
    numpy, 76
    pandas, 106
SUM() (MySQL function), 53
sums
    aggregating data, 53, 110
    cumulative, 76, 107
    numpy, 76
    partial, 82, 178
supernodes, 126
supervised learning, 157
support vector machines (SVN), 159
SVD (singular value decomposition), 43
SVN (support vector machines), 159
swapaxes(), 68
symmetric distribution, 150
synonym sets, 39
synonyms, 39
synsets, 39
synthetic sine wave, generating, 80

T
\t, regular expressions, 21
T attribute, transposing arrays, 67
T==data, 67
tables, *see also* frames
    altering, 50

creating in MySQL, 48
deleting records, 50, 52
dropping, 49
extracting from web
pages, 118
inserting records, 50–51
joining, 54
tabs, removing, 10
tabular data, *see also* CSV
files; numerical tabular data
format, 5
reading with pandas, 116
tabular numeric data,
see numerical tabular data
tagged data
file fragments, 32
finding tags, 32
format, 5
part-of-speech (POS) tagging, 42
removing tags, 32
tags
file fragments, 32
finding, 32
HTML, 30–31
hyperlink tags, 32
part-of-speech (POS) tagging, 42
processing HTML/XML
files, 30–33
removing in BeautifulSoup,
32
structure in BeautifulSoup,
32
XML, 31
tail(), 88, 90
testing data, 158, 170
text classification, 38, 43
text data, 29–45
about, 1, 29
formats, 5
handling CSV files, 34
HTML file processing, 30–
33
natural language processing, 38–43
projects, 44
reading JSON files, 36
reading and saving arrays, 79
TEXT data type, 49
TextFileReader, chunking, 118
thousands, 116
threshold, sampling, 126
tick_params(), 138

tight_layout(), 138
time
databases, 49, 51
datetime parsing, 116
TIME data type, 49
time series processing, 2
TIMESTAMP data type, 49
timestamps, MySQL databases, 49
TINYINT data type, 49
TINYTEXT data type, 49
title(), 138
TN (true negative), 158
to_csv(), 117
tokenization, 38, 41
top na_option, 106
TP (true positive), 158
training data, 157–158, 170
transforming data, pandas,
109–115
transpose(), 68
transposing, numpy, 66–67
trigonometry, universal functions, 73
triple double quotes ("""), xv
triple quotes ('''), xv
true negative (TN), 158
true positive (TP), 158
tuples
defined, 13
multiindexes, 95
Twitter, 36
type inference, 116
type narrowing, 66

U

U.S. Census Bureau
aggregating data by mapping, 111
merging data example,
101
plotting project, 146
state similarity calculator
project, 82
U.S. Higher Education
Dataset, 82
ufuncs, *see* universal functions
undirected graphs, 122, 130
Unicode and plots, 141
uniform(), 152

uniform distribution, 148,
152
Uniform Resource Identifiers
(URIs), MongoDB, 57
unimodal distribution, 150
union, 78
union1d(), 78
unique(), 78, 108
UNIQUE constraint, 50–51
United States Department of
Agriculture (USDA), 156
universal functions
pandas, 109
round(), 72
using, 72–73, 76, 109
unparsing, URLs, 19
unpickling data, 27
unstack(), 96
unstructured data, *see* natural language processing
(NLP)
unsupervised learning, 157
UPDATE, 52
upper(), 10
uppercase
converting in normalization, 41
converting strings, 10
stop words, 41
URIs, MongoDB, 57
urllib.parse, 19, 23
urllib.request, 19
urlopen(), 19
urlparse(), 19
URLs
handle, 19
hyperlink tags, 32
opening, 19
parsing, 19, 23
regular expressions, 23
urlunparse(parts), 20
USDA (United States Department of Agriculture), 156

V

value_counts(), 108
values
counting, 108
creating dictionaries, 14
dictionary data structure,
13
frames, 88
imputing, 100
JSON objects, 36

replacing, 100
series, 86
sorting frames and series
by, 105
values attribute, series, 86
var(), aggregating data, 110
VARCHAR data type, 49
variables
aggregating data, 110
discretization, 112–114
dummy, 113
scaling for k-means clus-
tering, 166
variance
defined, 150
linear regression, 160–
165
vectorized operations,
see numpy, broadcasting
vectorized universal functions, see universal functions
versions, modules, xv
visualization, see graphs;
plotting
Voronoi cells, 168
vseq, 14

W
\W, regular expressions, 21
\w, regular expressions, 21
walks, graph, 123
weakly_connected_components(),
131
weather vs. alcohol consumption project, 119
web crawling, recursive, 33
weighted graphs, 122–123
weights, graph edges, 122–
123
WHERE, 53
where() method, 75
whiskers, plots with, 139
whitespaces
regular expressions, 21
removing, 10–11, 34
widths parameter, reading
fixed-width data with pandas,
118
Wikimedia project, 44

Wikipedia
building network exam-
ple, 127
project, 44
wildcards, globbing, 26
William of Ockham, 29, 112
with statement, 18
word frequency counter, 28,
40, 175
word tokenization, 38, 41
word_tokenize(), 41
WordNet, 39
wordnet corpus, 39
WordNetLemmatizer, 42
WordPunctTokenizer, 41, 61, 176
words
boundaries, 21
creating copora, 40
frequency, 28, 40, 43,
175
lemmatization, 42
segmentation, 43
splitting strings with regular expressions, 23
stemming, 41
tokenization, 38, 41
words corpus, 38
words corpus, 38
words() method, creating copora, 40
WorldWideWebSize, 19
write(), 18
write(line), 18
write_adjlist(), 133
write_edgelist(), 133
write_gml(), 133
write_graphml(), 133
write_pajek(), 133
writelines(ines), 18
writerow(), 35
writerows(), 35
writing
CSV files, 34
CSV files with pandas, 117
data with pandas, 85
files, 18, 27
network analysis, 133

X
X axis
descriptive statistics, 106

plotting, 137, 140
swapping in arrays, 68
x value of sigmoid, 163
x*, regular expressions, 21
x+, regular expressions, 21
x?, regular expressions, 21
xkcd() function, 141
xkcd plots, 141
xlabel(), 138
xlim(), 140
XML
as data format, 5
compared to HTML, 31
defining tags, 31
parsing with BeautifulSoup,
31
processing files, 30–33
xml.parser, 31
xscale(), 140
XSLT (eXtensible Stylesheet
Language Transformation),
31
xticks(), 138
xyplot(), 135
x{2,5}, regular expressions, 21
x{2}, regular expressions, 21
x|y, regular expressions, 21

Y
\y, regular expressions, 21
Y axis
descriptive statistics, 106
plotting, 137, 140
swapping in arrays, 68
Yahoo! Finance, 156, 161,
181
Yahoo! Weather, 36
ylabel(), 138
ylim(), 140
yscale(), 140
yticks(), 138

Z
zeros(), 65
zip(), 14
Zipf distribution, 149
zipping, saving arrays, 79

Long Live the Command Line!

Use tmux and Vim for incredible mouse-free productivity.

tmux

Your mouse is slowing you down. The time you spend context switching between your editor and your consoles eats away at your productivity. Take control of your environment with tmux, a terminal multiplexer that you can tailor to your workflow. Learn how to customize, script, and leverage tmux's unique abilities and keep your fingers on your keyboard's home row.

Brian P. Hogan
(88 pages) ISBN: 9781934356968. $16.25
https://pragprog.com/book/bhtmux

Practical Vim, Second Edition

Vim is a fast and efficient text editor that will make you a faster and more efficient developer. It's available on almost every OS, and if you master the techniques in this book, you'll never need another text editor. In more than 120 Vim tips, you'll quickly learn the editor's core functionality and tackle your trickiest editing and writing tasks. This beloved bestseller has been revised and updated to Vim 7.4 and includes three brand-new tips and five fully revised tips.

Drew Neil
(354 pages) ISBN: 9781680501278. $29
https://pragprog.com/book/dnvim2

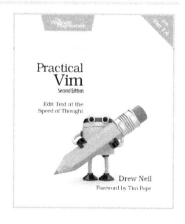

Secure and Better JavaScript

Secure your Node applications and make writing JavaScript easier and more productive.

Secure Your Node.js Web Application

Cyber-criminals have your web applications in their crosshairs. They search for and exploit common security mistakes in your web application to steal user data. Learn how you can secure your Node.js applications, database and web server to avoid these security holes. Discover the primary attack vectors against web applications, and implement security best practices and effective countermeasures. Coding securely will make you a stronger web developer and analyst, and you'll protect your users.

Karl Düüna
(230 pages) ISBN: 9781680500851. $36
https://pragprog.com/book/kdnodesec

CoffeeScript

Over the last five years, CoffeeScript has taken the web development world by storm. With the humble motto "It's just JavaScript," CoffeeScript provides all the power of the JavaScript language in a friendly and elegant package. This extensively revised and updated new edition includes an all-new project to demonstrate CoffeeScript in action, both in the browser and on a Node.js server. There's no faster way to learn to write a modern web application.

Trevor Burnham
(124 pages) ISBN: 9781941222263. $29
https://pragprog.com/book/tbcoffee2

The Joy of Mazes and Math

Rediscover the joy and fascinating weirdness of mazes and pure mathematics.

Mazes for Programmers

A book on mazes? Seriously?

Yes!

Not because you spend your day creating mazes, or because you particularly like solving mazes.

But because it's fun. Remember when programming used to be fun? This book takes you back to those days when you were starting to program, and you wanted to make your code do things, draw things, and solve puzzles. It's fun because it lets you explore and grow your code, and reminds you how it feels to just think.

Sometimes it feels like you live your life in a maze of twisty little passages, all alike. Now you can code your way out.

Jamis Buck
(286 pages) ISBN: 9781680500554. $38
https://pragprog.com/book/jbmaze

Good Math

Mathematics is beautiful—and it can be fun and exciting as well as practical. *Good Math* is your guide to some of the most intriguing topics from two thousand years of mathematics: from Egyptian fractions to Turing machines; from the real meaning of numbers to proof trees, group symmetry, and mechanical computation. If you've ever wondered what lay beyond the proofs you struggled to complete in high school geometry, or what limits the capabilities of the computer on your desk, this is the book for you.

Mark C. Chu-Carroll
(282 pages) ISBN: 9781937785338. $34
https://pragprog.com/book/mcmath

Pragmatic Programming

We'll show you how to be more pragmatic and effective, for new code and old.

Your Code as a Crime Scene

Jack the Ripper and legacy codebases have more in common than you'd think. Inspired by forensic psychology methods, this book teaches you strategies to predict the future of your codebase, assess refactoring direction, and understand how your team influences the design. With its unique blend of forensic psychology and code analysis, this book arms you with the strategies you need, no matter what programming language you use.

Adam Tornhill
(218 pages) ISBN: 9781680500387. $36
https://pragprog.com/book/atcrime

The Nature of Software Development

You need to get value from your software project. You need it "free, now, and perfect." We can't get you there, but we can help you get to "cheaper, sooner, and better." This book leads you from the desire for value down to the specific activities that help good Agile projects deliver better software sooner, and at a lower cost. Using simple sketches and a few words, the author invites you to follow his path of learning and understanding from a half century of software development and from his engagement with Agile methods from their very beginning.

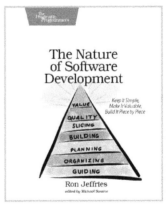

Ron Jeffries
(178 pages) ISBN: 9781941222379. $24
https://pragprog.com/book/rjnsd

The Pragmatic Bookshelf

The Pragmatic Bookshelf features books written by developers for developers. The titles continue the well-known Pragmatic Programmer style and continue to garner awards and rave reviews. As development gets more and more difficult, the Pragmatic Programmers will be there with more titles and products to help you stay on top of your game.

Visit Us Online

This Book's Home Page
https://pragprog.com/book/dzpyds
Source code from this book, errata, and other resources. Come give us feedback, too!

Register for Updates
https://pragprog.com/updates
Be notified when updates and new books become available.

Join the Community
https://pragprog.com/community
Read our weblogs, join our online discussions, participate in our mailing list, interact with our wiki, and benefit from the experience of other Pragmatic Programmers.

New and Noteworthy
https://pragprog.com/news
Check out the latest pragmatic developments, new titles and other offerings.

Save on the eBook

Save on the eBook versions of this title. Owning the paper version of this book entitles you to purchase the electronic versions at a terrific discount.

PDFs are great for carrying around on your laptop—they are hyperlinked, have color, and are fully searchable. Most titles are also available for the iPhone and iPod touch, Amazon Kindle, and other popular e-book readers.

Buy now at *https://pragprog.com/coupon*

Contact Us

Online Orders:	*https://pragprog.com/catalog*
Customer Service:	*support@pragprog.com*
International Rights:	*translations@pragprog.com*
Academic Use:	*academic@pragprog.com*
Write for Us:	*http://write-for-us.pragprog.com*
Or Call:	+1 800-699-7764